A GUIDE TO THE CLASSICAL COLLECTIONS

OF CORNELL UNIVERSITY

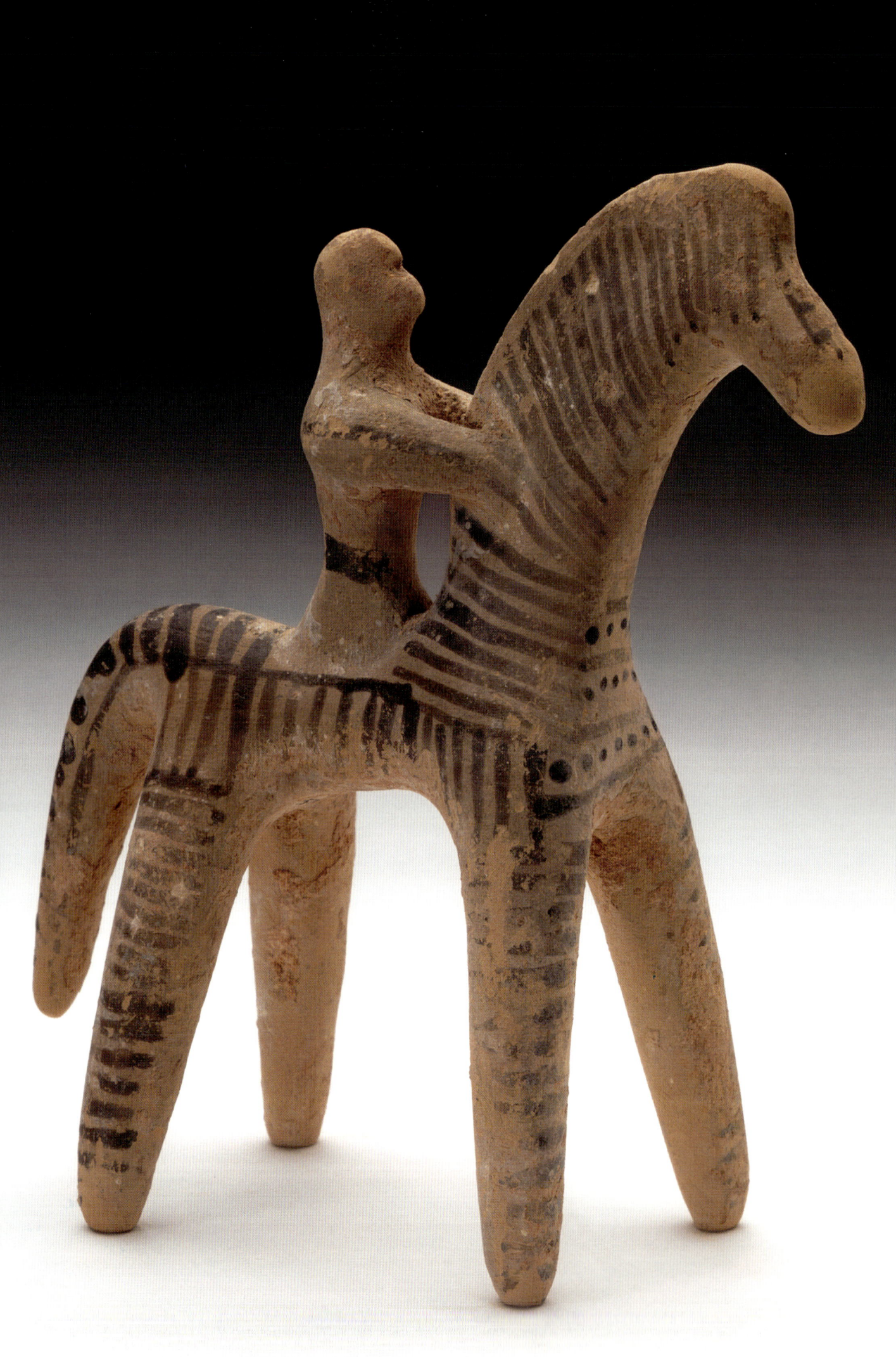

A Guide to the
Classical Collections
of Cornell University

BY

Peter I. Kuniholm

Nancy H. Ramage

Andrew Ramage

EDITED BY

Jane S. Terrell

HERBERT F. JOHNSON MUSEUM OF ART
CORNELL UNIVERSITY

CORNELL UNIVERSITY PRESS
ITHACA, NEW YORK

ARCHAEOLOGY & ART PUBLICATIONS
RICHMOND, INDIANA

Second Printing with updates, October 2010

FRONT COVER:
Palmyra, Syria
Funerary Monument [detail]
2nd-3rd century A.D.
Limestone
Gift of Genevieve and Richard Tucker
2002.021

INSIDE FRONT AND BACK COVER:
The Sage Collection of casts in
Goldwin Smith Hall

Photographs of artwork by the Johnson
Museum Digital Access Project
(Matthew Ferrari and Michael Holobosky)

The publication costs of this volume
have been partially underwritten
by the Laistner Endowment of *Cornell
Studies in Classical Philology* and by
the Hull Memorial Publication Fund of
Cornell University.

Published by:
Herbert F. Johnson Museum of Art
Cornell University
Ithaca, New York 14853
www.museum.cornell.edu

Printed in Turkey by:
Mega Print

Distributed by:
Cornell University Press
Ithaca, New York 14850
www.cornellpress.cornell.edu

Archaeology & Art Publications
Richmond, Indiana 47375
www.aapbl.com

CONTENTS

FOREWORD

FROM THE RELENTLESSLY forward-looking perspective of the twenty-first century, it is easy to ignore the antecedents of our culture and to forget how much of modern life derives from the poets, philosophers, and artists of antiquity. Yet we are indebted to the ancients for many of the fundamental ideas that underlie Western democracy and for many of the aesthetic principles that still govern our conception and appreciation of art.

Cornell is fortunate that its first president, Andrew Dickson White, believed it essential for a first-rate university to have a strong collection of ancient art on campus. President White made numerous trips to Europe to purchase works of art and to commission plaster casts of classical statuary for his new university (just as, for instance, he purchased superb literary materials in French for Cornell's library).

In addition, several early members of Cornell's faculty were excellent archaeologists and art historians who understood the value to students of seeing, analyzing, copying, and working with original classical art. They developed a tendency at Cornell to merge the theoretical and the practical, to provide students with opportunities for hands-on learning, and thus advanced Ezra Cornell's vision of a university where the classical tradition and the applied and "mechanic" arts could coexist and even enhance each other.

Over the years, Cornell's collection of classical art has been dispersed into many buildings across campus and has thus lost much of its impact on students, faculty, staff, and visitors. The publication of this handbook will help remedy this situation by providing a useful compendium.

With this guide, students and scholars can locate the impressive plaster casts made from classical Greek and Roman statues and other pieces that were brought to Cornell by A. D. White. They can also search out sculptures, pottery, coins, and functional objects from the ancient world that have been added to Cornell's collections over the years. Many of these antiquities are of high quality and significance. They are invaluable for research and scholarship and for teaching present day students in fields from classics to art history to Near Eastern studies, anthropology, and city and regional planning.

I am delighted that Peter I. Kuniholm, Professor of Archaeology and Dendrochronology, Andrew Ramage, Professor of the History of Art and Archaeology, Nancy H. Ramage, Charles A. Dana Professor of the Humanities and Arts, and Professor of Art History at Ithaca College, and Jane S. Terrell, a recent Cornell graduate, have compiled this *Guide to the Classical Collections of Cornell University* in conjunction with the Herbert F. Johnson Museum of Art. The guide provides an intimate handbook to Cornell's antiquities and a valuable lens through which to view some of the wonders of the ancient world, and it is my hope that it will lead you to take an educational tour of Cornell's collection.

HUNTER R. RAWLINGS III
President and Professor of Classics
Cornell University

ACKNOWLEDGMENTS

T HE CLASSICAL WORLD has been an inextricable part of Cornell since its beginning, not just because of the name Ithaca (one of the many cities in New York State named for their Greek and Roman counterparts), but also because Andrew Dickson White, the University's founding President, was deeply aware of the fundamental importance of classical history and culture, and how it has shaped our values and ways of thinking today.

Happily, this awareness has continued into the twenty-first century, and we are grateful to Hunter R. Rawlings III, a classical scholar and Cornell's president, for his perceptive and enthusiastic Foreword. The University is fortunate in having many classicists on its faculty, and two of them, Peter Kuniholm and Andrew Ramage, and Professor Nancy H. Ramage of Ithaca College, have devoted many hours to writing this volume and preparing it for publication. We are deeply grateful to these three dedicated colleagues.

We are equally grateful to Jane S. Terrell, a recent art history and archaeology major who has supervised this project with great energy and expertise. Elaine Engst at Cornell University Library's Division of Rare and Manuscript Collections was as always enthusiastic and unfailingly helpful in tracking down images of Cornell's classical collections in use. On the Museum staff, Andrew Weislogel has worked with Ms. Terrell and the faculty members on the publication, Matthew Ferrari has taken the excellent digital images, and Catherine Davidson has once again helped to edit the publication, worked with the designers, and seen it through the press.

Finally, but not least, we are grateful to the generous donors of the works discussed and reproduced here. Without their help, we would not have had these objects, which make the ancient world real and relevant to generation after generation of students.

FRANKLIN W. ROBINSON
The Richard J. Schwartz Director
Herbert F. Johnson Museum of Art

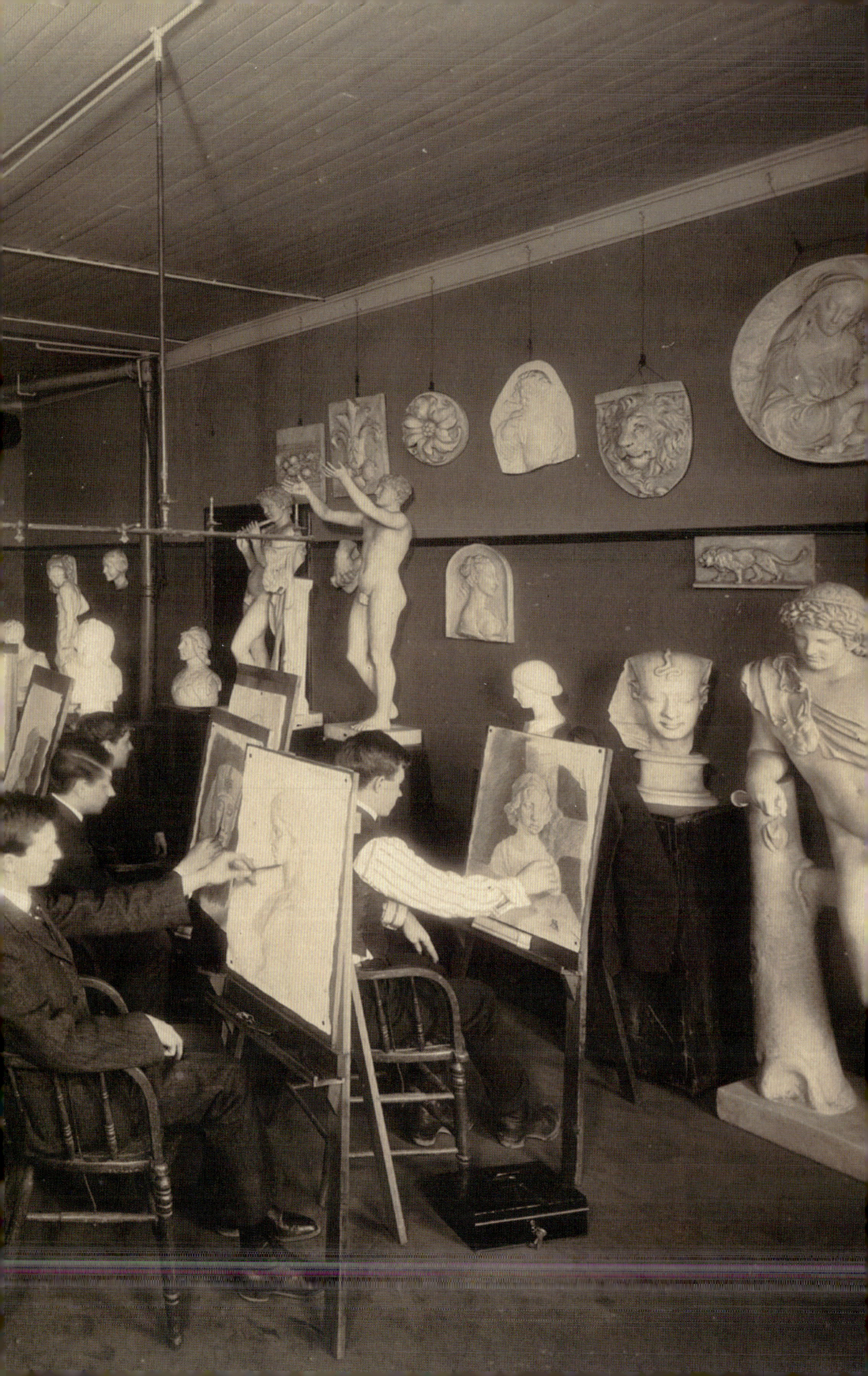

INTRODUCTION

Brief History of the Collections

From practically the opening day of the new university in Ithaca in 1865 its founders, administrators, and professors of classical studies sought to augment the standard nineteenth century menu of Latin and Greek languages and literatures with the archaeology of both Greece and Rome and with copies or models of classical antiquities, and sometimes with the antiquities themselves. The notion seems to have been that since travel to Europe was expensive and beyond most students' budgets, Cornell would endeavor to bring classical antiquity to Ithaca, New York. As E. B. White, Class of 1921, said in "I'd send my son to Cornell," an often-reprinted essay: "Cornell is in Ithaca, N.Y., where Greek meets Indian. The name of the town is Greek, the statues in the basement of Goldwin Smith Hall are Greek,..."

The first major influx of classical material to Cornell consisted of hundreds of plaster casts of Greek and Roman statuary, selected by Andrew Dickson White and paid for by Henry Sage (thus "The Sage Collection"). At one time these amounted to some 631 major pieces of sculpture including about 150 running feet of frieze, several metopes, and most of the surviving pedimental sculptures from the Parthenon in Athens. Also represented were architectural sculptures from the Zeus Temple at Olympia and many others, as well as free-standing sculptures such as the Laocoon group, the Charioteer of Delphi, the Tenea Kouros, the statue of Athena Lemnia, which A. D. White assembled from its fragments in Dresden and Bologna, the Aphrodite of Knidos, the Farnese Hercules, the Doryphoros, dozens of statues of muses and busts of emperors, and about 2,000 copies of gems, seals, and medals in the Berlin Museum and the university museums of Germany. The latter collection is in the A. D. White Reading Room of Uris Library. For the current location of a number of the large statues, well-known to generations of Cornellians, see the *Stroller's Companion to Classical Art on the Cornell Campus* at the end of this introduction.

The collection included architectural elements of every sort: profiles of moldings, cornices, and capitals so that beginning architecture students could learn the "school figures." Old photographs of Cornell show introductory art or architecture classes sketching in front of the casts in the old Beaux Arts tradition (fig. 1).

Fig. 1;
Early Cornell students in a drawing class learn to sketch by studying plaster casts of ancient sculpture. Photo: Division of Rare and Manuscript Collections, Cornell University Library.

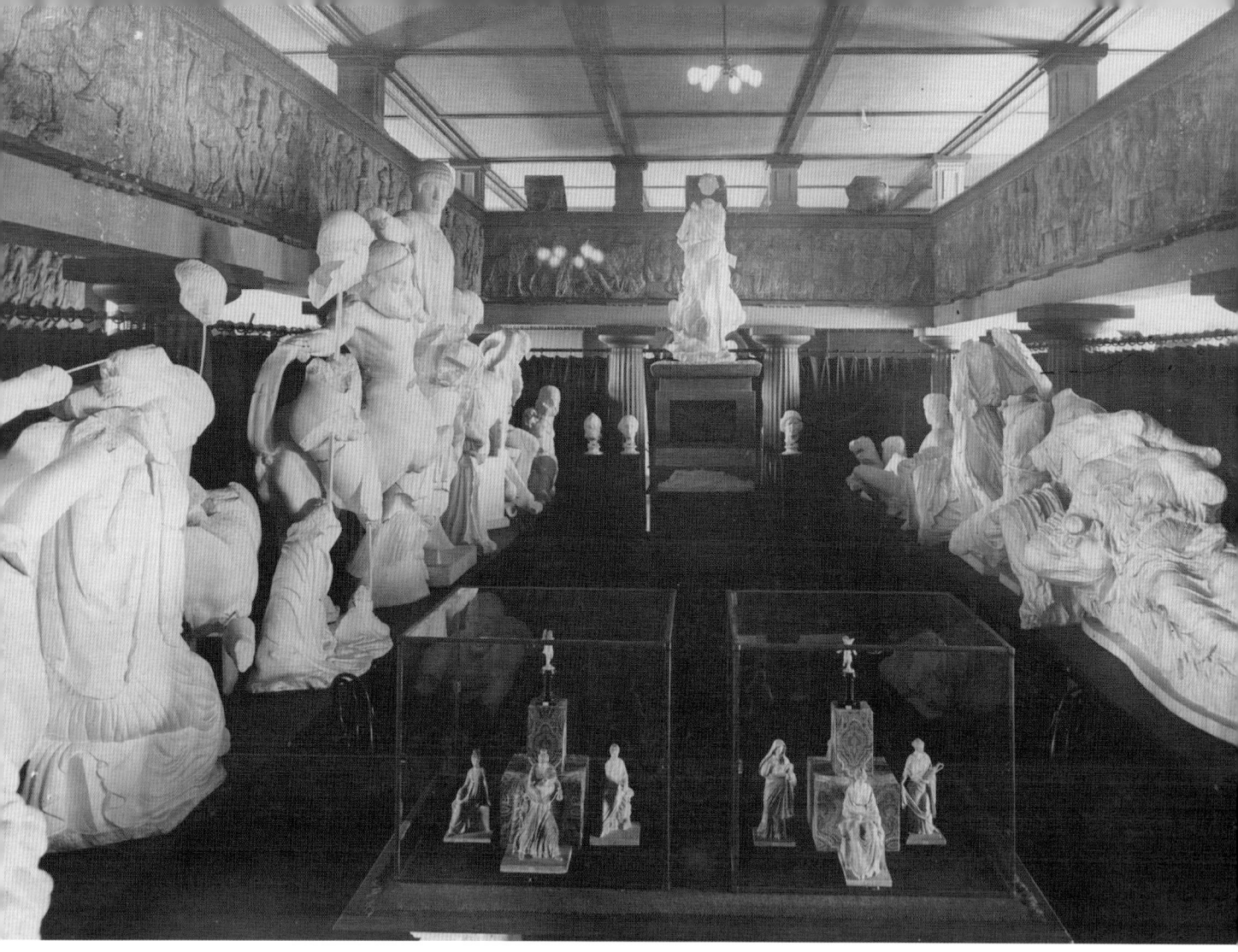

A collection of copies of Tanagra figurines was named in honor
of Mrs. A. D. White. Other collections included electrotypes of
all the important Greek coins in the British Museum collection
acquired for the [Cornell] Archaeology Museum in 1903, copies
of the more significant metal objects from the Shaft Graves at
Mycenae, and the first-ever electrotype copy of a major statue,
Myron's Discobolos, now on display in the west entry to
Goldwin Smith Hall. In short, almost every significant statue
that was in European collections in the late nineteenth century
was copied at A. D. White's request, and the copy was brought
to Ithaca. (All of this is to say that more than a century ago edu-
cators were well aware of the effectiveness of teaching aids.)
Newspapers of the time comment on how the annual shipment of
statuary had just arrived and was undergoing the necessary
repairs prior to installation. Later on, Greek and Roman coins,
Hellenistic and Roman papyri from the Fayyum, tomb groups
from Abydos (with Sir Flinders Petrie's handwriting still on the
tickets), inscriptions, cuneiform tablets, mosaics, and a good part
of the Greek and Roman tableware from Antioch were added to
the Cornell classical collections.

A Wandering Museum:
from McGraw to the Johnson with stops in between

In 1891 the entire basement of McGraw Hall – some 5,000
square feet – was given over to the casts. When the Museum of
Casts in McGraw opened formally in 1894 (fig. 3), the story
made newspaper headlines. *The New York Times* ran an article
that said: "As a museum of classical sculpture the collection is
actually excelled by no other university museum in the United
States, and among other foundations only by the Museum of
Fine Arts of Boston." Staff members at the *Cornell Daily Sun*
claim to have found an old Baedeker guide to North America
which gave Ithaca a star on the strength of the cast collection
alone. Old photographs show that a Doric entablature was built
so that visitors could see the casts in their proper architectural
setting. McGraw Hall even had a room painted in the Pompeian
Fourth Style, currently hidden under an anonymous coat of off-
white paint.

In 1906 the cast collection was moved to Goldwin Smith
Hall (fig. 2) where it occupied the entire basement, with rooms
(now faculty offices) on the Ground Floor corridor marked on
old building plans as "Coin Room," "Inscriptions Room," "Small
Bronze Room," and the like.

The home of the collections from 1953 until the building of
the Herbert F. Johnson Museum in 1973 was the Andrew Dickson
White House. When the Johnson opened, there was clearly not
enough room for everything classical, and much of the collection
in the A. D. White House was dispersed. Selene's horse from the
Parthenon pediment that gazes out over the first floor is the lone
cast from the Sage Collection currently in the Museum.

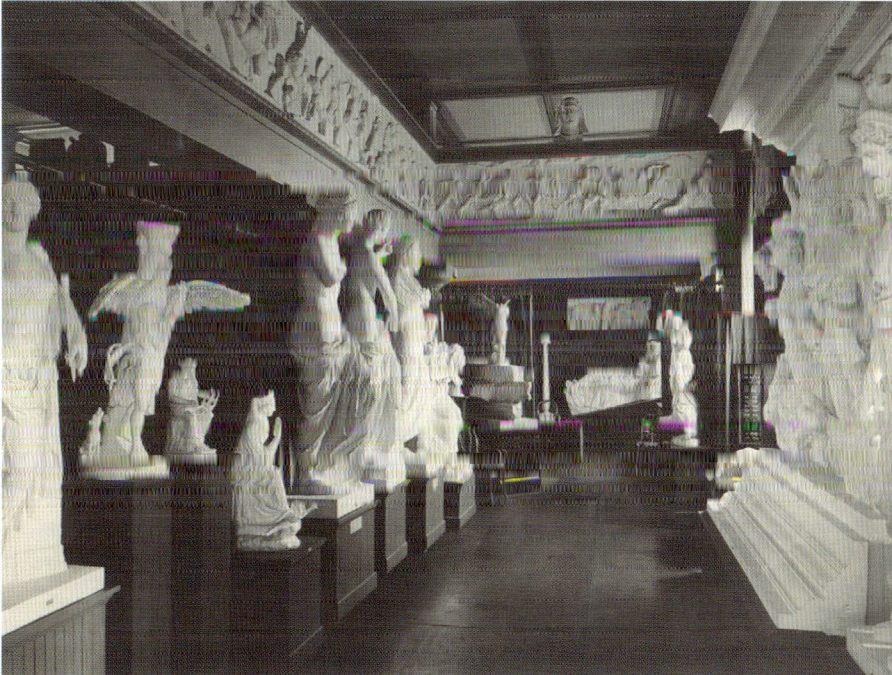

Fig. 3:
The Museum of Casts, McGraw Hall.
Photo: Division of Rare and
Manuscript Collections, Cornell
University Library.

People: the Early Archaeologists and Curators of the Collections

Alfred Emerson, the first scholar and curator to put together a catalogue of the classical cast collection sometime between 1891 and 1897, notes that he had found a sculptor who was willing to copy and bring to Ithaca the entire sculptural program of the Parthenon "for the modest sum of $25,000." At a time when a skilled mechanic earned $2 a week, a sum of $25,000 can hardly be called modest! Our predecessors took their classical archaeology seriously, and expense appears not to have been an issue.

Another early Cornell classical archaeologist who left material that is still in usable condition in the Olin Library archives was Eugene Plumb Andrews, who, hanging from a rope over the gable of the Parthenon in Athens in 1896 (fig. 4), made paper squeezes, or impressions, of the dowel holes from an inscription in bronze letters which he was able to decipher as Latin rather than Greek. The inscription was put up on the Parthenon by the emperor Nero and was probably ripped off shortly after Nero's death by an unappreciative Athenian population. Wilhelm Dörpfeld, the Director of the German Archaeological Institute in Athens, took pity on young Andrews as he swung back and forth on his rope in the January wind and provided him with a proper boatswain's chair. As the transfer to the new equipment was made, Andrews discovered that all but one strand of his rope had frayed through and that he had come close to being a squeeze himself. Andrews stayed on at Cornell until 1936 as professor of archaeology and curator of the Museum of Casts.

Even more important legacies are the squeeze collections left by the remarkable classical archaeologist J. R. Sitlington Sterrett (at Cornell 1901–1914). A large number of Attic and Anatolian inscriptions, the Greek and Roman texts of the *Res Gestae Divi Augusti* or *Monumentum Ancyranum* (1907), and the first-ever corpus of inscriptions of what was then called hieroglyphic Hittite, now called Luvian (collected in 1907 and published promptly in 1911) are still available for study, many of them in much better shape than the original stones from which they were copied. Just before the Great War, Sterrett went on a crusade to found an institute to study the monuments and cultures of Asia Minor and the Near East. He wrote a proposal, asking for $100,000 a year for survey, excavation, study, and publication of the results. The program was to last for 20 years. Sterrett solicited dozens of university presidents, deans, and professors to endorse his letter, but then he died of a stroke in 1914. James Henry Breasted took essentially the same proposal as Sterrett's, put it before the newly-founded Rockefeller Foundation, and as a result the world-famous Oriental Institute is in Chicago rather than in Ithaca.

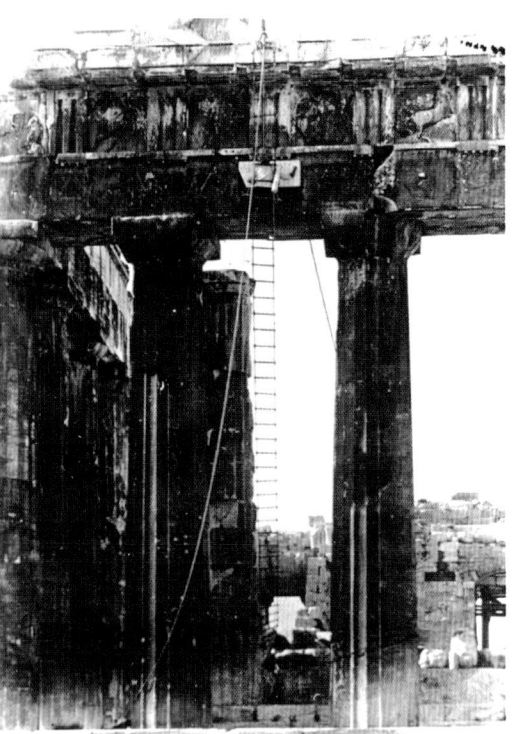

Fig. 4:
Cornell archaeologist
E. P. Andrews hangs from
the Parthenon to decipher
what remains of an
inscription in 1896.
Photo: Division of Rare and
Manuscript Collections,
Cornell University Library.

A classical archaeologist who left a major imprint on Cornell, if not a directly-attributable set of artifacts, was Benjamin Ide Wheeler, at Cornell from 1886–1899, later President of the University of California at Berkeley. We suspect that some 400 of the Greek squeezes in the collection were made by him since the pencilled identifications are from a system current in the late 1880's. Gertrude Bell, in her *The Thousand and One Churches*, comments about encountering the Cornell Expedition under Albert ten Eyck Olmstead (Cornell B.A., M.A., Ph.D.), assiduously studying thousands of potsherds. When Olmstead left Cornell for the University of Chicago, presumably the pottery went with him, for we have never found a sherd directly attributable to this expedition.

Frederick Waagé, at Cornell from 1938 to 1972, excavated at Antioch, then in Syria, now in Turkey, in the 1930s and brought significant quantities of material to Ithaca for study and publication. The custom of the time was that at the close of the excavation all the archaeological finds were divided into three piles. The government representative had the first choice, the excavator the second, and the land-owner the third. Usually the latter was only too happy to sell his pile to whoever would pay the most money for it. We are still sorting through the objects that Waagé brought back over 60 years ago. Waagé also made regular purchases of coins, some of which are depicted in this guide, to add to a collection that clearly began well before his arrival on campus. Subsequently, alumni and friends made additional gifts or bequests to augment the collection of approximately 3,000 coins.

In 1958 Harvard's George Hanfmann and Cornell's Henry Detweiler began a collaboration at the huge archaeological site of Sardis in Lydia (Turkey)

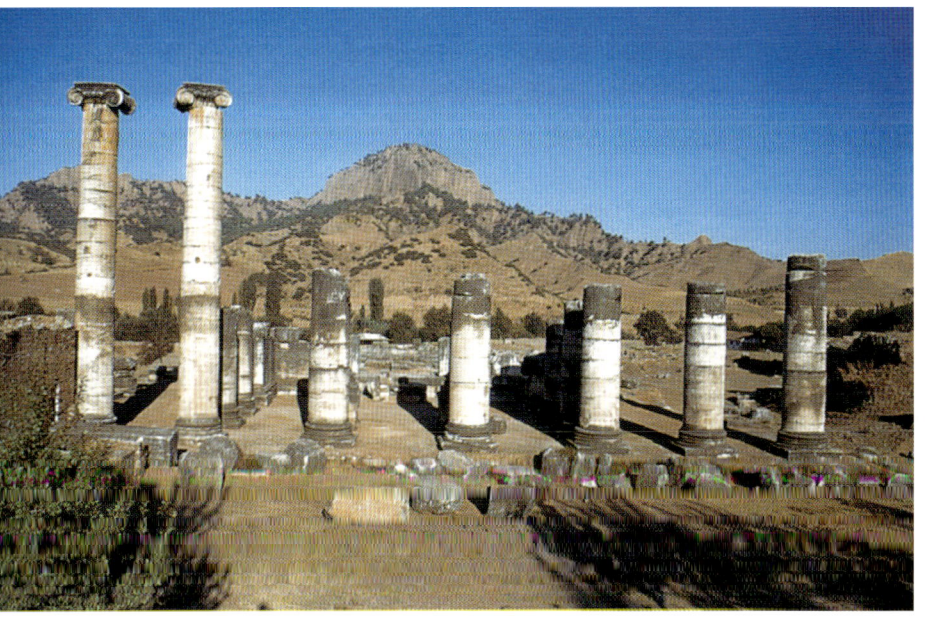

Fig. 3:
The Temple of Artemis and the Necropolis at the site of ancient Sardis. Photo: Archaeological Exploration of Sardis.

where the Harvard-Cornell excavations continue under a new generation of excavators, including Associate Director Andrew Ramage, one of the authors of this guide. Because Turkish law prohibits the export of antiquities, a special Sardis show of photographs and drawings was on exhibit in the Johnson Museum in 1984, and every year a number of Cornell students spend their summers working at the University's longest-running excavation project. The fieldwork and publication thus go hand-in-hand with the study and display of the objects. One example which preceded this guide was Ramage's class project: *Emblems of Authority: Greek and Roman Coins from Two Alumni Collections*, which was written to accompany a show at the Johnson Museum in 1994.

Since 1976 another of the authors of this guide, Peter Kuniholm, has conducted a course on "basement archaeology" in which several hundred Cornell undergraduates have taken time out from the work of the dendrochronology laboratory to find, identify, rehabilitate, and prepare for exhibition several hundred of the old casts. We are making progress, although lack of formal exhibition space continues to be a serious hindrance. The third author, Nancy H. Ramage, who also participated for many years in the Sardis Expedition, has been working with her students at Ithaca College on a group of nineteenth century plaster casts of ancient and Renaissance sculptural works that are on long-term loan from The Metropolitan Museum of Art.

What is in this guide and why

The two dozen classical objects that the visitor to Cornell sees on display in the Johnson Museum and the many more that we celebrate in the pages of this guide are, thus, a selected fraction of our holdings. They have been culled from perhaps 12,000 items, the fruits of 140 years of collection and accumulation by Cornell archaeologists, some well-known, others not, and by alumni and friends of Cornell. Where we know the names of the donors, we cite them in the catalogue. Some donors, particularly for many of the coins, must often be classified as 'anonymous' because of the lack of a continuous set of records, especially from the years before the Museum's founding. However, in recent years the Abrams, Caldwell, Ostrander, Robinson, Salton, Simpson, Theodorou, Tucker and Wunsch families have made significant gifts, and these are acknowledged in the catalogue.

Not everything that is excavated at an archaeological site is either museum-quality or even vaguely photogenic. Study material, whether exhibitable or not, is valuable, nevertheless, for both pedagogical and scholarly purposes, but a problem at Cornell and universities elsewhere has always been where to display it. Compounding the problem had been changes in the early 1960s: a) the invention of the 35mm. slide (which neither needed constant dusting nor took up as much space as the plaster casts), and b) an aesthetic taste that said that only 'originals' were worth having. Casts, according to the criteria of 40 years ago, were by definition 'fakes' (and therefore 'bad') and were best destroyed. In the 1960s, Harvard, Yale, and Princeton, for instance, tossed out their cast collections. Fortunately, while Cornell went though a similar phase, it was not as thoroughly completed as at some of the other universities. About half of

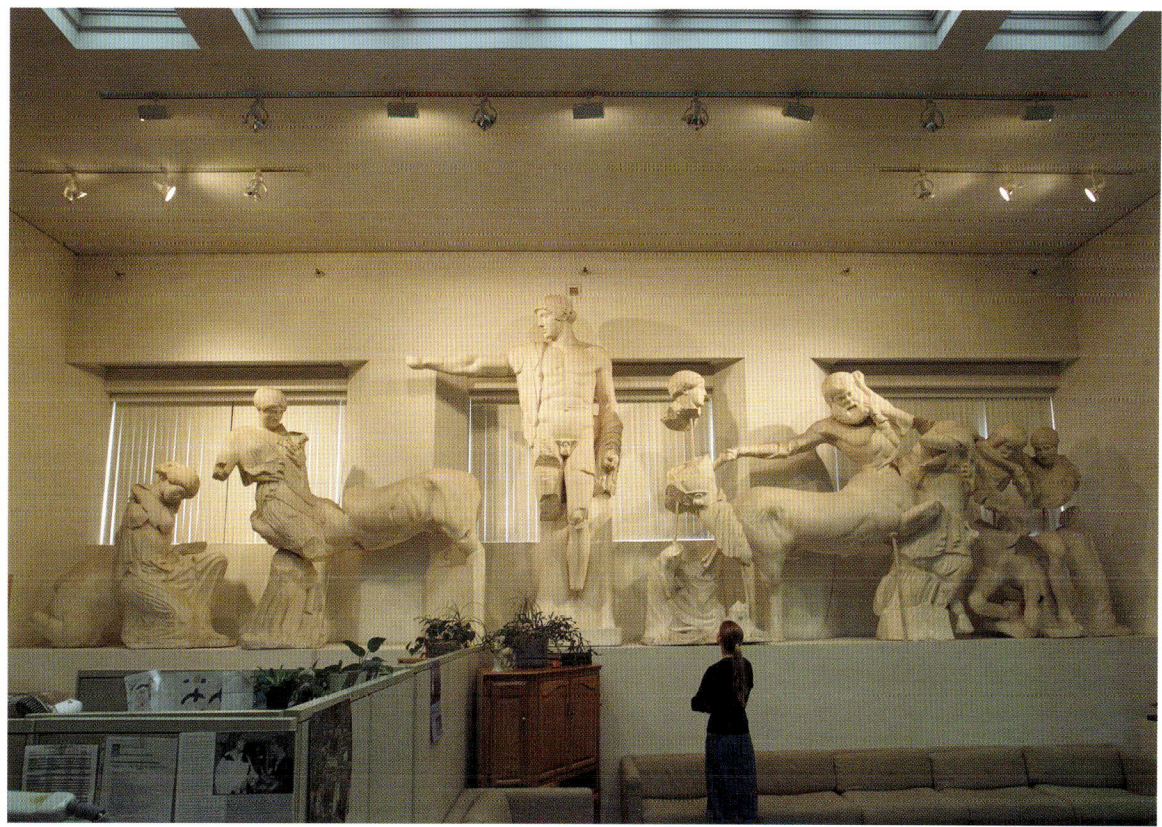

Fig. 6:
Casts of pedimental sculptures from the Temple of Zeus at Olympia decorate the Admissions Office in 172 Goldwin Smith Hall. Photo: Frank DiMeo/University Photography.

what we had was destroyed or given away, and it is the survivors of this once-proud collection that may be seen in classrooms, libraries, and administrative and faculty offices around campus (Fig. 6). Indeed, newcomers to Ithaca are often unaware that there ever was a formal collection. Accordingly, we decided it was high time to take stock of what we have on campus and to publish a guide to this small selection of some of the more interesting classical antiquities at Cornell University, both in the Johnson Museum and elsewhere on campus.

How one might think one's way through a guide like this

In this survey of the Cornell collections almost every class of material object from the classical world except architecture and large-scale painting is represented. From an enormous area encompassing Etruria in the west, Bactria and Parthia in the east, Macedon in the north, and Ptolemaic Egypt in the south, across a timescale of some 1,400 years from the eighth century B.C. to the sixth century A.D. To begin with, then, we are trying to cover an extraordinary amount of both space and time, and we have deliberately avoided limiting our focus to, say, fifth century B.C. Athens and Augustan Rome. Moreover, we know a lot about some of our objects and very little about others. This variation in the amount and quality of background information illustrates at once part of the intrigue, puzzle, satisfaction, and—sometimes—frustration of classical archaeology.

We can occasionally glean gratifying amounts of precise information from a single object. The manufacture of some of the coins, for example, can be pinned down to a year, or even within a year, if the B (*beta*) on the amphora on which the owl is standing on the Athenian New Style Tetradrachm (no. 32) represents the second month of the year 164/3 B.C., as we believe. The head of Athena along with her owl depict the patron goddess of the city, and the olives, olive leaves, and oil amphora depict Attica's chief export. We are also told the names of the archons or magistrates of the year. Other coins, however, although they bear the name of a known city, may be dated only to within a century or two at best.

Similarly, some of the pottery, the Athenian black-figure plate (no. 3), for example, was probably produced in Athens between 560–540 B.C. Furthermore, we think we know the name of the pot painter, a certain Lydos, who, with a name like that, had to have been born in Lydia in western Asia Minor. Other pottery is less diagnostic. We are able only to specify a century or two, and a general location such as Greece, Cyprus, or Etruria.

The two funeral inscriptions range from informative to enigmatic. The grave stele from Asia Minor (no. 19) tells us the names of the young deceased and of his surviving wife, and precisely what he was doing for the emperor—making an official journey—when he died. The Etruscan cinerary urn (no. 18) on the other hand, gives us an initial and two names, none of which tells us very much at all.

Some of the objects were intended to be "works of art" as we think of the term today. Others are the mundane objects of daily life. But one thing is clear: the makers and painters of these objects knew their mythology. They knew who belonged in a scene and who did not, and it is to be presumed that their customers were equally knowledgeable. Thus even we, removed by a couple of millennia, are able to identify representations of divinities, persons, or events that we know about from the surviving texts. Mythological, literary, and historical references enliven many of the depictions: Zeus, Athena, Apollo, Aphrodite, Menelaos, Helen, possibly Electra and Orestes, Augustus, the emblems of the Greek city-states such as the labyrinth at Knossos or the owl at Athens or Pegasus at Corinth, and the victories and sometimes grandiose titles of the Roman emperors.

The sculptors who carved the hard bronze dies on which the coins were struck also had to be able to carve hundreds of them with no significant variation. Augustus tells us in the *Res Gestae Divi Augusti* how he spent many hundreds of millions of sesterces on various public works. Even if the payments were in gold aurei, that still meant a lot of die-cutting, and the resulting images had to be immediately recognizable so that the coins could be legal tender all across the Roman world. The task of producing these coins is just as impressive as the emperor's claimed deeds.

Artists/craftsmen did make mistakes, on occasion. The carver of the grave stele inscription miscalculated his available space and tried to cram everything into the last lines (and over the border) of the tablet.

Some of the objects were expensive, even in their time. We know that in the fifth century B.C. a drachma was a day's wage for a working man, so one of our tetradrachms was worth four days' wages back then. One of the Ptolemaic gold octadrachms from the third century would have been worth about 104 days' wages, or somewhat less if one makes an allowance for inflation. Look at the white-ground lekythos (oil jar), both the object itself (no. 4) and the depiction of similar lekythoi on the Attic red-figure pelike (no. 7). We can only guess at how much such a vase might have cost the grieving family who needed oil containers to make appropriate remembrances at the funeral, although some modern scholars deny that pots were all that expensive. Was all the artistic embellishment necessary? Clearly, somebody thought it was, or else we would find only undecorated oil jars in the cemeteries. We see, then, that these objects were 'special' — significant enough for their purchasers to go to some trouble, if not expense, to buy them for the funeral of a family member.

What is particularly fascinating to the authors of this guide, all of whom have worked on the fringes of the Greek and Roman world, is the way in which the Greek and Roman cultures and forms of artistic expression were adopted and imitated, not always successfully, in the lands to both east and west. This explains in part some of our selections for the catalogue. The easiest way to see this is on the coins, where, beginning with Alexander the Great (no. 39), and continuing on in the Bactrian and Parthian issues (no. 47, 50, 51), we see representations which appear Greek with the odd additions of the horns of Ammon, or an elephant cap complete with tusks, and an occasionally bungled inscription consisting of little more than punched dots with connecting lines. The engraver of the latter coin clearly was unfamiliar with his Greek. In the west the early Roman Republican issues look much more Greek than the crude lumps of copper which had been the Romans' earliest money. At the end of the Roman Empire, the Byzantine Emperors kept the Roman tradition alive, with clearly derivative portraits and symbols and legends for another thousand years.

PIK

STROLLER'S COMPANION TO CLASSICAL ART ON THE CORNELL CAMPUS

Unless otherwise noted, these objects are from the H. W. Sage Cast Collection.

The Arts Quad

IN SIBLEY HALL
Sleeping Ariadne, Louvre (long known by Cornell custodians as the "Purple Lady")

Fine Arts Library:
Hera (dedicated by Cheramyes on Samos), Metope from Selinus of Perseus slaying the Gorgon Medusa, Capitoline Aphrodite of Capua, Venus de Milo, etc.

IN THE FOUNDRY
The Laocoon

IN GOLDWIN SMITH HALL

West entrance
Delphi Charioteer, Discobolos, Athenia Lemnia, Jason Seley's automobile-bumper copy of the "Hellenistic Ruler"

South entrance
Aegina, Temple of Aphaia, pedimental figures

Basement
Art History Dept.:
Doryphoros, Agias from Delphi

Room No. B-48, Classical Collections Seminar Room and Work-Room/ Dendrochronology Lab: Bust of Mausolus, Attic Relief, the "Beautiful Head" from Pergamon, figure from the Theatre of Dionysos, Lansdowne Amazon Head, Head from Olympia Zeus Temple Pediment, miscellaneous figurines, Giant from the Pergamon Altar, small statuettes, Electrotypes of the British Museum Collection of Greek Coins

Ground Floor
Room No. G-55, Advising Center: Tenea Kouros, Acropolis No. 674, Dying Gaul and other Pergamene statues, more Parthenon frieze slabs, Roman amphora, the Capitoline Dionysos, the Belvedere Torso, busts of Demosthenes, Demeter, and Doryphoros

Corridor Vitrines:
Tanagra Figurines, Bust of Nefertiti, Archaic Hera from Olympia, Hypnos, Sappho, Homer, Pericles, Augustus, Euripides, Demeter from Knidos, Demetrios Poliorcetes, figures from Trajan's Column, two heads of Augustus, Ottonian ivories, Tanagra figurines

Art History Office: Nike Temple Parapet, Sandalbinder and other figures

Temple of Zeus coffee shop:
More Parthenon Frieze slabs

First Floor
Room No. 122, 124: more Parthenon Frieze slabs, various inscriptions

Room No. 135: Aphrodite of Knidos, Colossal Roman Foot, Torso of a young Apollo, bilingual inscription from Antiphellos

Room No. 147, Dean's Office:
Parthenon Frieze slabs

Room No. 172, Admissions Office: Temple of Zeus Pediment from Olympia, Marcus Aurelius, the Piombino Apollo

Second Floor
corridor:
Bassae Frieze

IN THE JOHNSON MUSEUM

First Floor
Selene's horse from the Parthenon

A variety of ancient objects from the classical collection can be seen on the first floor of the museum; more from the classical collection can be seen by making an appointment with the curatorial department.

Agriculture Quad

IN MANN LIBRARY

Room No. 500:
Antiochus Soter, Berlin

Central Campus

IN MYRON TAYLOR HALL, LAW SCHOOL

The Gortyn Law Code

AT THE STATLER HOTEL

Outside on the north patio:
Hercules II– Jason Seley's
automobile-bumper copy of the
Farnese Hercules

IN URIS LIBRARY

Andrew Dickson White
Reading Room:
cabinet with approx. 2000 casts of
coins, gems, and medals

Reading Room:
Marble head of the young Augustus.
Bronze and marble head of the young
Marcus Aurelius

PIK & JST

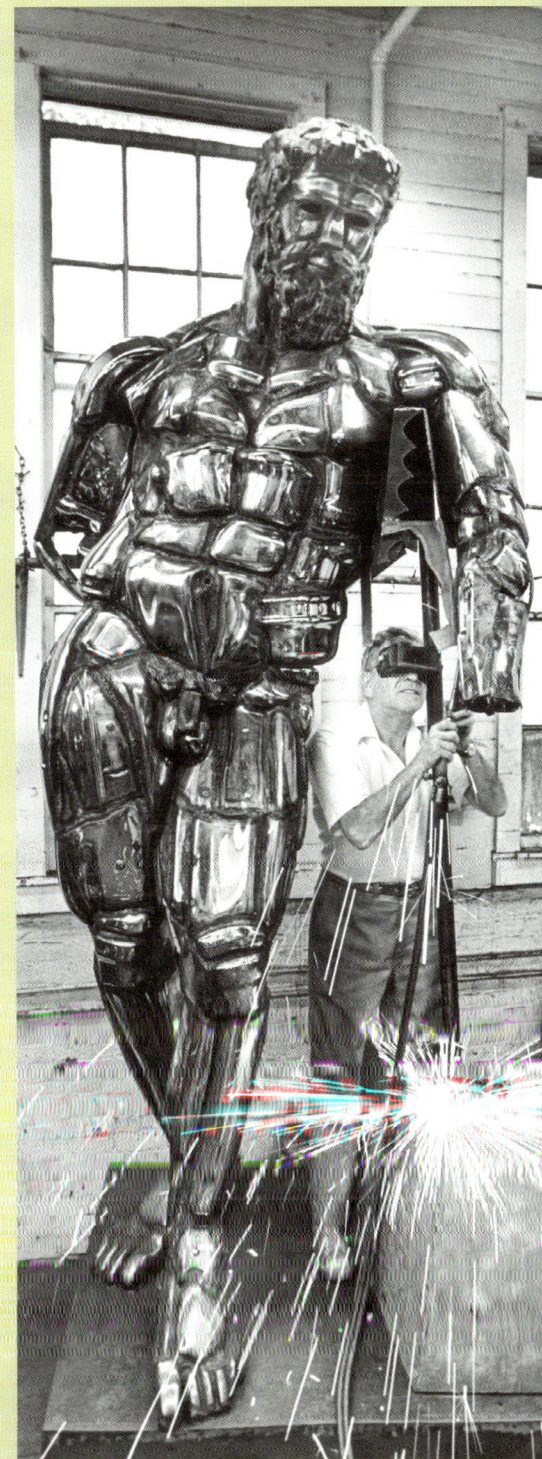

*Fig. 7
Professor Jason Seley welding ordinary car bumpers into a
rendition of the famous Farnese
Herculean. Seley gave the
university the sculpture, aptly
named "Herakles at Ithaka."
Jon Reis Photography.*

*Note: These statues have a tendency
to migrate from one semester
to another. If you cannot find
something, just ask.*

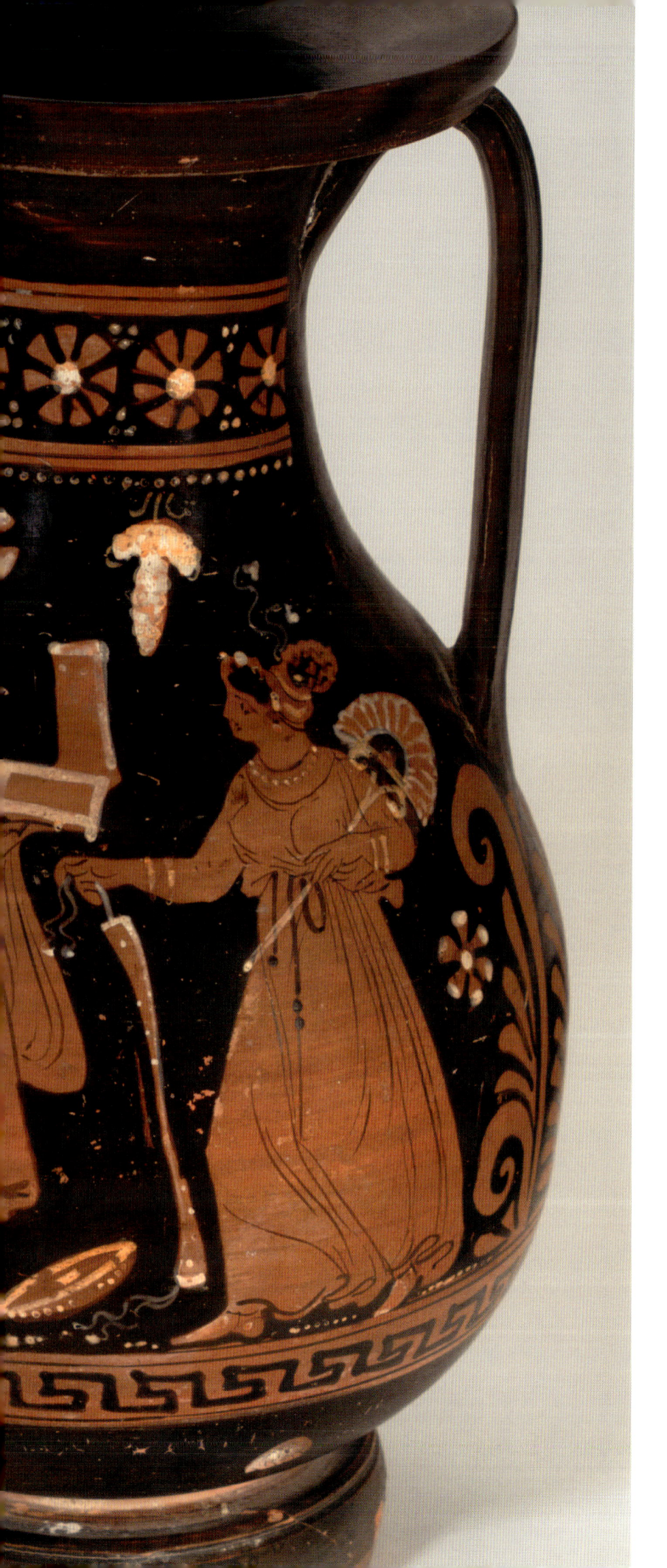

POTTERY

THE POTTERY THAT FOLLOWS comes from various parts of the Greek and Roman world. The interest in these pieces lies in many different features, ranging from the techniques used, to the shapes of the pots, to the subject matter represented in the painted decoration.

To examine just a few points here: the Greek, Etruscan, and Roman potters all used the wheel to make their pots. The clay varied, of course, from place to place; thus clay from Athens is a reddish color, while that from Cyprus is tannish. Most potters used a black glaze (richer and shinier in some places than others), and sometimes they used other colors, such as red, purple, or white to supplement the decoration.

Geometric pottery is so-called because the linear painted decoration on the pots is based primarily on geometric designs. At Cornell we also have examples of other ways of decorating pots, used throughout the Greek world in later centuries, including black-figure, red-figure, and white-ground pottery. Black-figure is distinguished (as the name suggests) by figures that are painted black, while the background is left the reddish color of the clay. Red-figure is a technique that basically reverses the effect: the figures are left the color of the clay, and the background is painted in solid black. In black-figure, interior decoration and details are incised; in red-figure they are painted. White-ground pottery is different: it is covered with a whitish paint (that unfortunately tends to flake off), and the figures are painted in a linear technique. One of the merits of white-ground painting is that often we are shown the colors of the various forms of dress.

The shapes of pots tell us a great deal about how they were used. To supplement the obvious differences, say, between a cup and a jug, there is other evidence, such as findspots, or literary references, that tell us which pots were used for funerals, weddings, or other occasions. On the other hand, many of the pots were in fact used in daily life, rather than for special events. Oil lamps (see no. 21) are in a class by themselves.

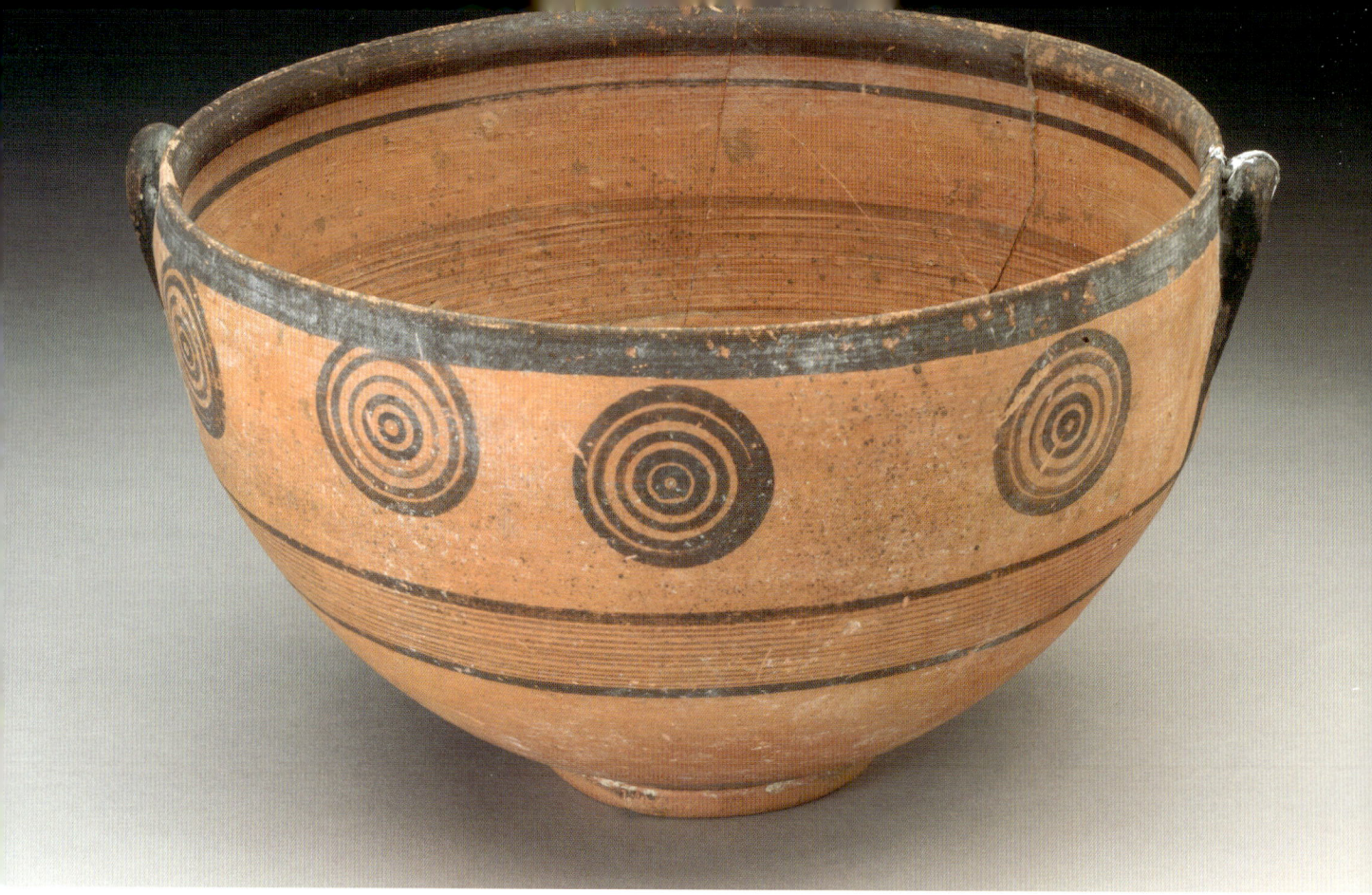

1.
Bowl with Handles,
ca. 700 B.C.

Cyprus

Ceramic. 12.7 x 22.8cm

Membership Purchase Fund.
77.023.010

Throughout Greek lands, from Athens to Cyprus, artists began around 1,000 B.C. to decorate their pottery with concentric circles, parallel lines, and other geometric designs. The concentric circles on this Cypriote bowl are made in the usual way: by a compass-like rotation using a multiple brush with five heads. The horizontal bands were easily applied by holding a brush still against the surface while turning the pot on the wheel. The handles, pressed tight against the sides, are hardly functional since one could get neither thumb nor finger through them; hence they are more for decoration in this case, or perhaps for hanging for storage by placing a string through the handles.

The lines and circles on this bowl are mechanically applied, and therefore look quite different from the freehand designs on the two Geometric horse figurines (nos. 16 and 17) of the same stylistic period.

PROVENANCE:
Purchased from the Cyprus Museum, Ministry of Communications and Works: Department of Antiquities, Nicosia, Cyprus.

NHR

2.

Bucchero Kantharos

Early sixth century B.C.

Etruria

Ceramic. 17.5 x 19.4 cm

Gift of Living Arts Foundation, Inc.
64.0004

The Etruscans specialized in a ceramic
ware that is black not only on the surface but also in the body of the clay.
They accomplished this by a "redu-
cing" atmosphere in the kiln, that is,
the burning up of all the oxygen in the
reddish clay which thus turns it black.

Bucchero pottery, as this type is
known, is imitative of metallic wares,
and is often burnished to a highly pol-
ished surface. The thin high handles,
with knobs at the top, are copied from
a metal cup, where handles like this
make more sense than in pottery,
where they are highly vulnerable to
breakage. A zig-zag decoration is
incised below the rim and filled with a
white chalky substance to bring out
the design. A graffito resembling the
Greek letter Λ (lambda), seen towards
the base, may indicate ownership of
the cup or may be an identifying mark
of the potter.

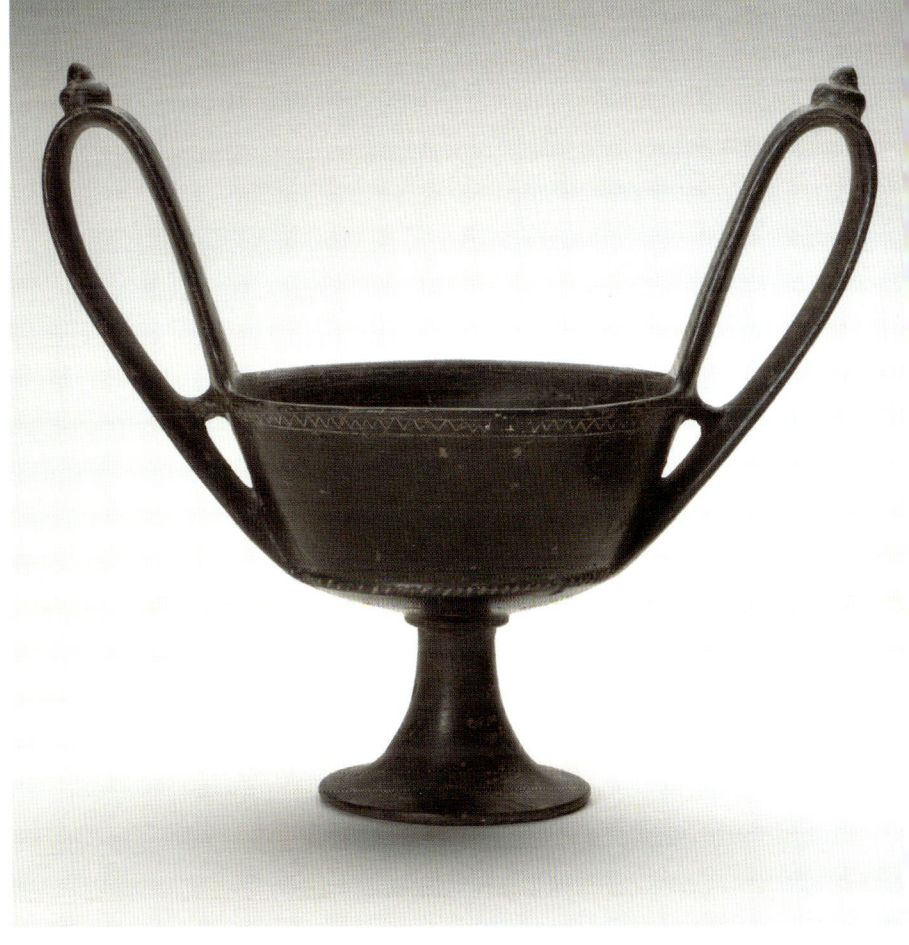

EXHIBITION HISTORY:
"Vessels: Stylistic and Functional
Reflections of the Ancient World,"
University Art Gallery, SUNY,
Binghamton, 10/20/78–11/19/78.

NHR

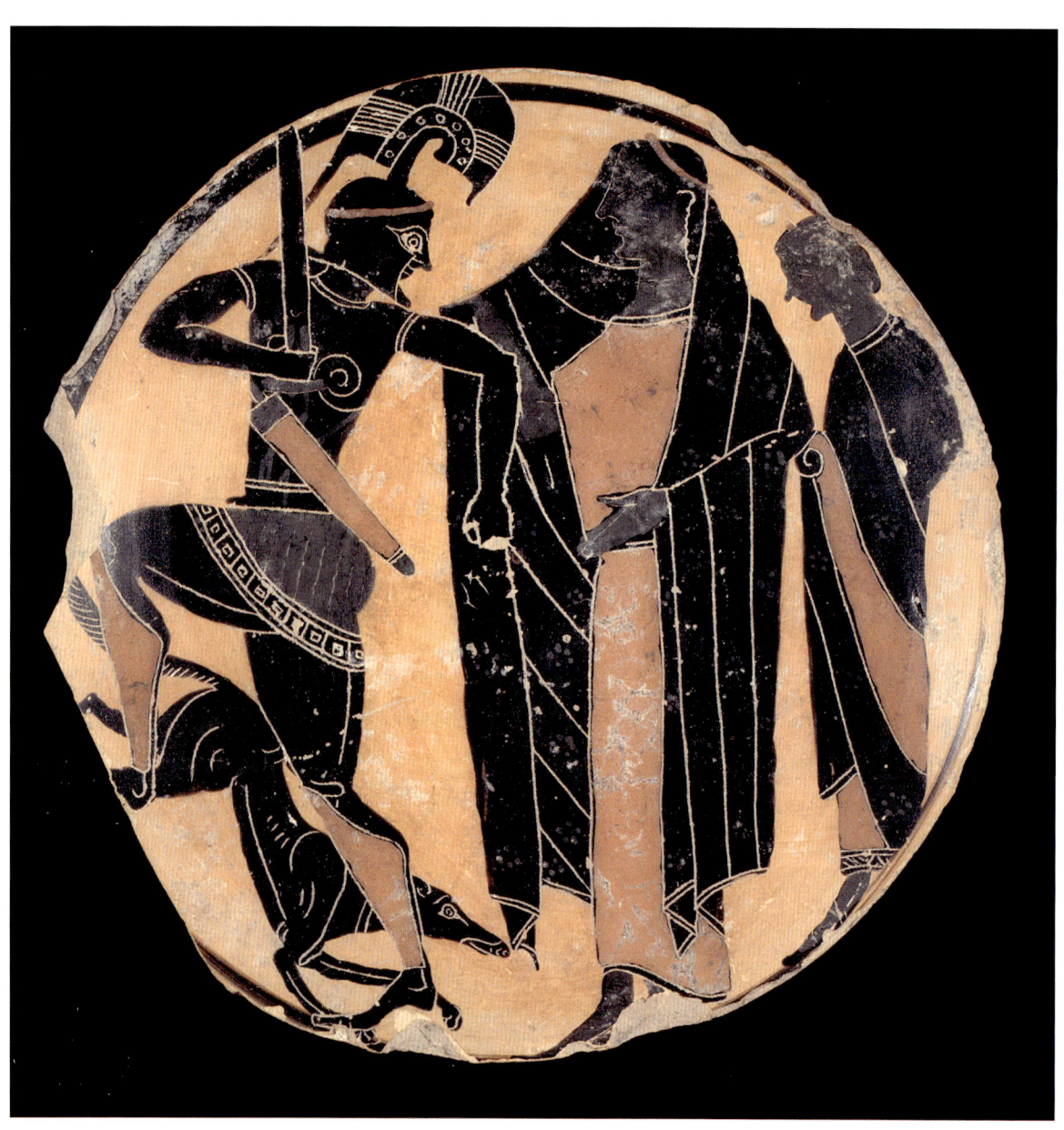

3.

Tondo from a Black-Figure Plate
"The Recovery of Helen by Menelaos"

Attributed to Lydos,
active 560–540 B.C.

Athens

Ceramic. Diameter: 14.9cm

Acquired through the generosity of the Class of 1930

The Frank and Rosa Rhodes Collection. 95.047

This piece was cut down at an unknown time, but originally served as the central part of a plate with a rim or collar.

The subject here is Menelaos taking back Helen after the Trojan War. The beautiful Greek Helen, with "the face that launched a thousand ships," (Marlowe, *Dr. Faustus*) had caused the Trojan War by deserting her husband Menelaos to become the lover of the Trojan prince, Paris. After the war, Menelaos intended to kill her, but, on seeing his beautiful wife once again, he fell back in love with her. We see him here at left, armed with a high crested helmet and greaves (armor for the lower legs), and still holding the sword with which he was going to stab her; but instead, he puts out his arm in a time-honored gesture of matrimony to lead her home. She, in turn, wears her mantle over her head, again in a ritualistic gesture that suggests matrimony. A servant at right bends her head, thus fitting nicely within the circular design. The dog sniffs eagerly at the hem of Helen's robe, recognizing his mistress. The lively movement depicted by Menelaos and the dog is sharply contrasted with the quiet dignity of Helen and the servant. In the sparest of artistic language the early Greek pot painter, Lydos, has managed to tell us a great deal about the story.

Both Helen and the female servant at right were originally painted white over their black skin, as can be seen by the grayish traces on their faces, hands, and feet. Painting female skin white was the normal practice in black-figure painting. Menelaos' kilt was also once painted white. The basic technique here, as in all black-figure pottery, is that the black glaze defines the figures, and other colors, like red, purple, and white, are added on top of the black. The details of the figures are incised into the clay with a sharp tool. The Athenian clay itself fires a warm orangey-red.

Note the use of the frontal eye on a profile face. This is a tradition that goes back to the Egyptians, and that lasted for hundreds of years. Another characteristic of vase painting of the sixth century B.C. was to make the chest and shoulders frontal, while the rest of the body is in profile. This is especially clear on Menelaos' body, and again is owed to Egyptian influence.

PUBLISHED:
Johnson Museum, 1998, p. 97.

NHR

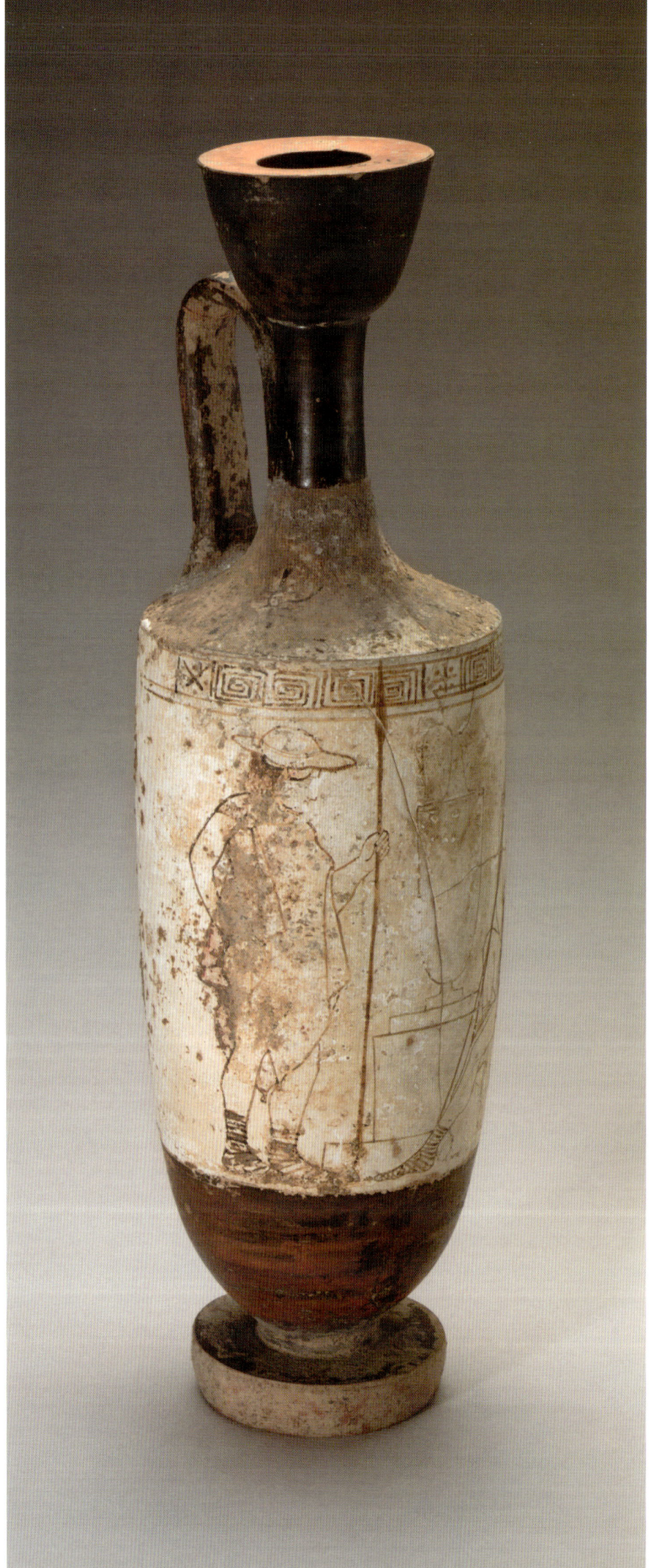

a.

4.

White-Ground Lekythos

ca. 450 B.C.

Athens

Ceramic. 32.39 x 9.53cm

Transfer from University Collections.
77.052

A seated and standing youth flank a
huge stone vase of the same shape as
the pottery vase itself—a lekythos—
which serves as a funerary monument
(no. 4b). This example may be the
earliest known representation of this
type of vase used to mark a grave,
and, if so, is an important benchmark
in the development of themes on
Greek vases.

   The man at left (no. 4a) wears a
traveler's cap with a broad, floppy
brim, a cloak that covers his body, and
sandals with thongs wrapped around
his ankles, and carries a spear. The
man at right (no. 4c), naked except for
cap and similar shoes, holds two
spears. A cloth lies over his upper
thigh, and covers the rock on which
he is sitting. This quiet and relaxed
scene may represent two deceased
men, which is unusual since normally
such subjects show a mourning
woman and a deceased man. It is an
appropriate subject for a lekythos,
however, which was frequently used
at grave sites in this period—the mid-
fifth century B.C.—and in the following decades. (See the examples on the
red-figure pelike, no. 7.)

   The agile painter, using sponta-
neous strokes of his brush, exhibits
the kind of lively drawing that is typical for this kind of vessel. The white
surface, covered with a thin layer of
white clay, called a "slip," provided
conditions akin to wall painting.

   The lekythos would have con-
tained oil with which men and women
would cleanse themselves. Thus, in a
funerary context, they were used by
the living and buried with the dead.
Large stone versions, like the one portrayed here (in 4b), but with relief
decorations, were commonly used for
grave monuments.

PUBLISHED:
Fairbanks, 1907, p. 208-210, fig. 46.

Kurtz, 1975, p. 62, 225, Pl. 53.

NHR

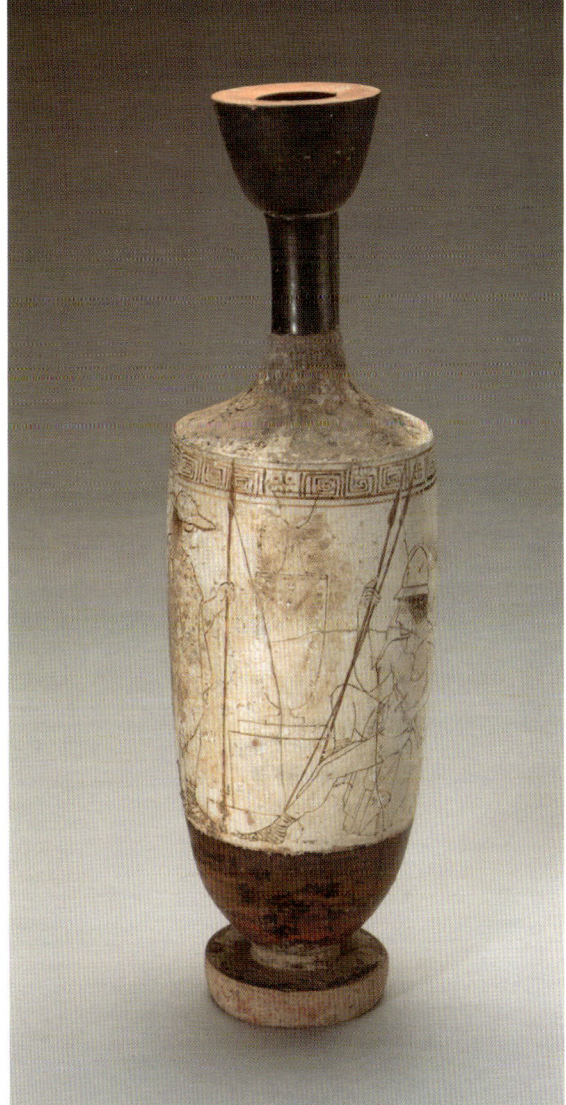

b.

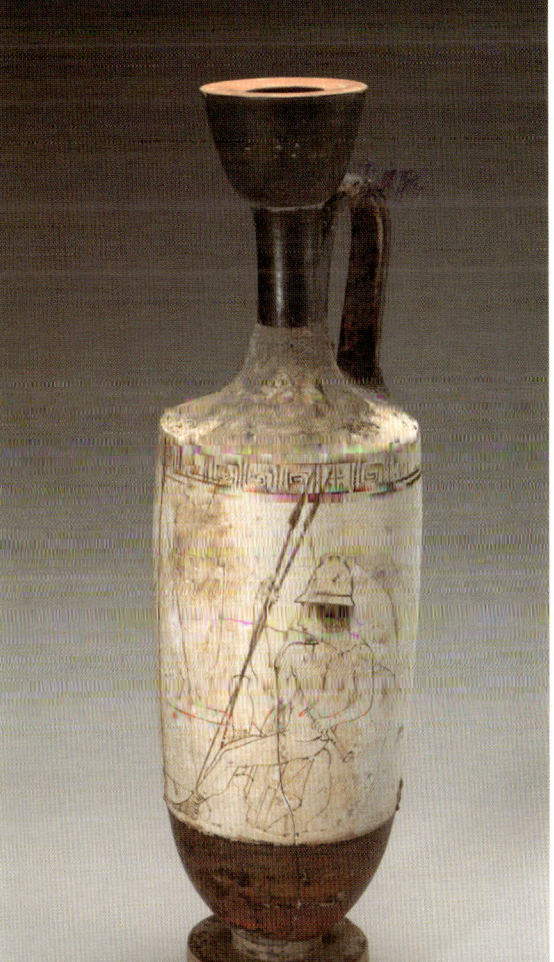

c.

Red-figure Pottery

The red-figure technique of Greek pottery, invented in Athens about 530 B.C., spread all over the Greek world, including the area called Magna Graecia (Southern Italy and Sicily). This manner of decorating pots allowed for much freer drawing than black-figure, as seen on the tondo (no. 3), and by the time of our pieces, late fifth and early fourth centuries B.C., artists had known for some time how to draw eyes in profile as well as bodies in three-quarter view. Drapery folds are more fluid, and the poses are more relaxed and realistic. The range of dilute glazes with which internal lines are painted allows for greater subtlety than the relatively cruder incision lines of the black-figure technique.

The following three vessels are all in the red-figure technique.

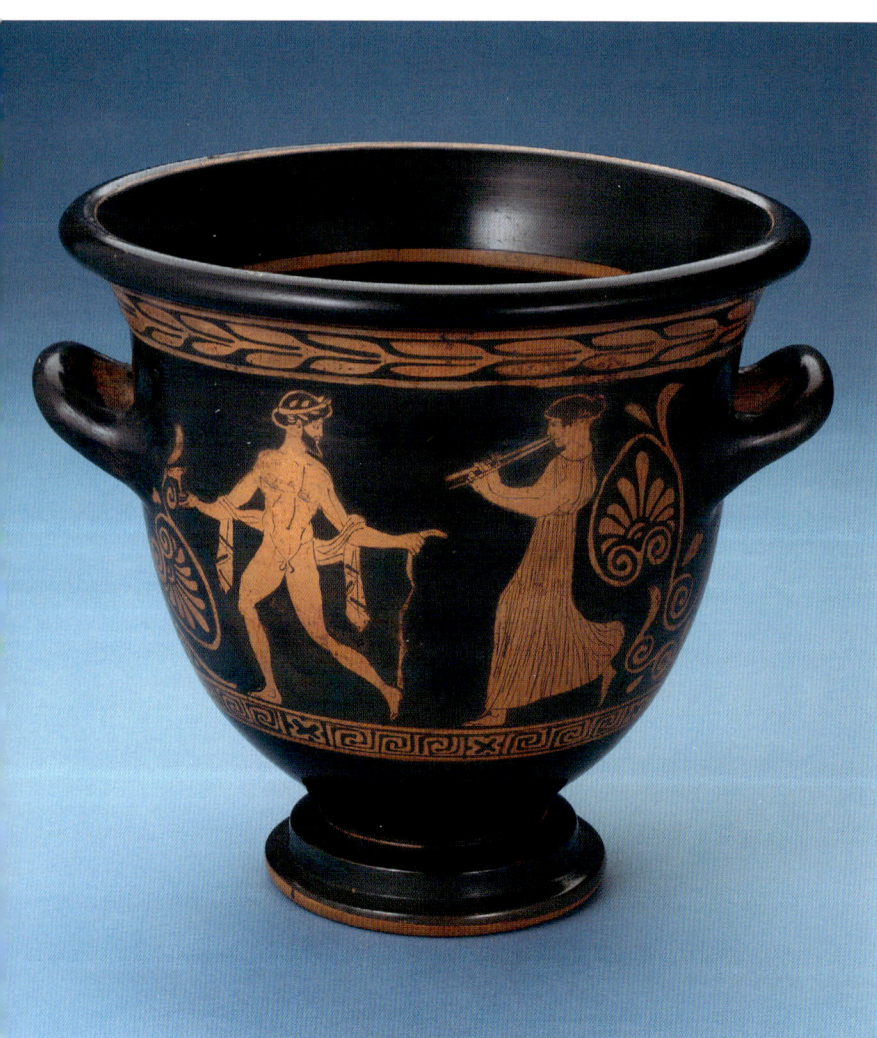

5.
Red-Figure Bell Krater
ca. 400 B.C.

Southern Italy

Ceramic. 19.05 x 20.65cm

Transfer from the History of Art Collection. 74.074.008

A bearded man with a crown of leaves runs to the left holding a drinking cup in his right hand and a staff in his left. He carries a cloth draped over his arms, leaving his body entirely naked. He turns back to look at the barefoot woman, perhaps a maenad, who follows him, playing the double-flute. She wears a flimsy dress called a chiton, made of thin crinkled material, and her hair is tied up in a kerchief. Notice that in this pot the woman seems to be chasing the man, who turns toward his pursuer, while on the Greek pelike (no. 7), Side B, the pursuit is initiated by the man.

A fine set of palmettes decorates the areas around the handles, and a horizontal border of leaves above and meander pattern below define the space of the pictorial scene.

NHR

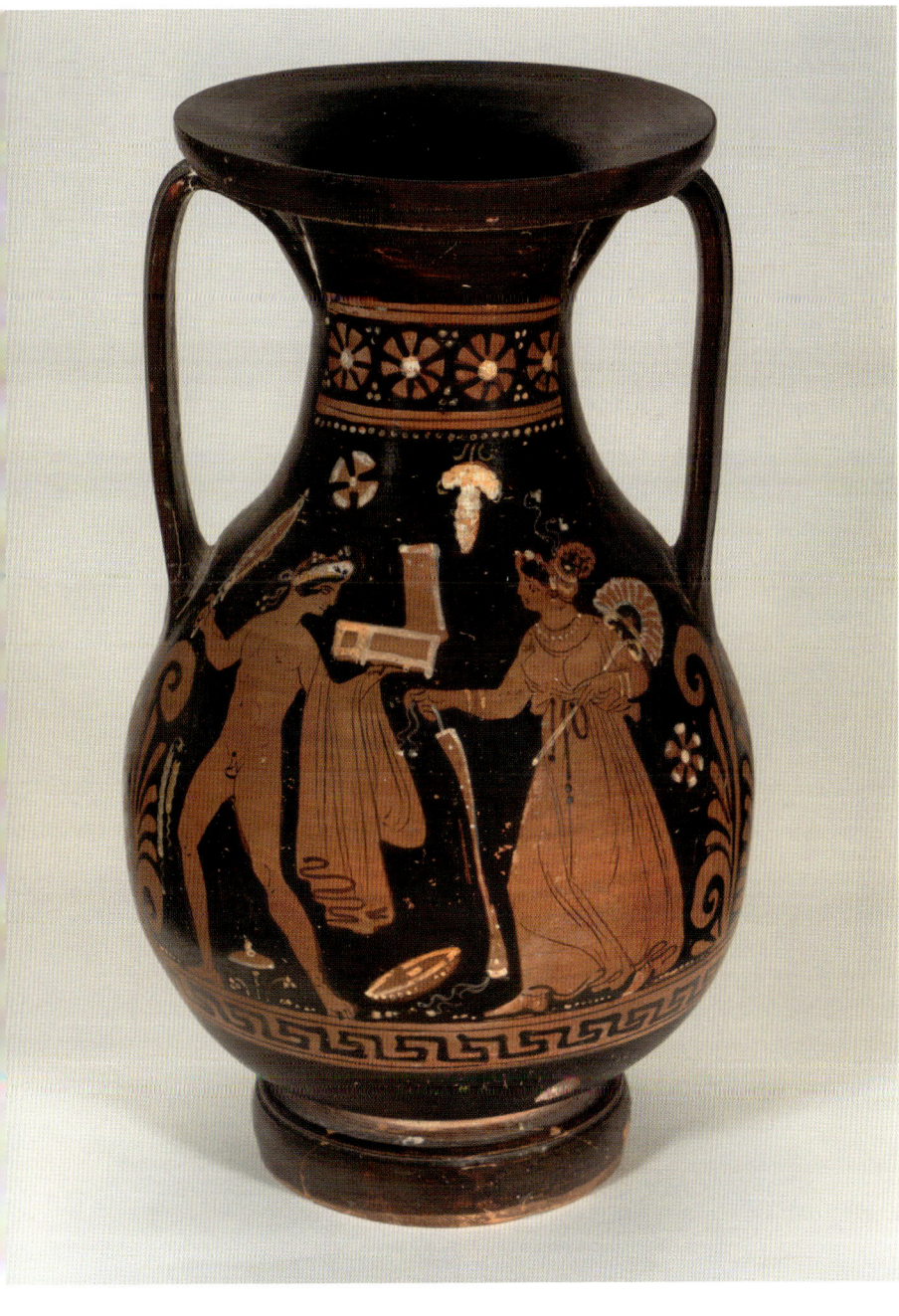

6.
Red-Figure Pelike
Fourth century B.C.

Apulia

Ceramic. 34 x 19.05cm

Bequest of David B. Goodstein,
Class of 54, by exchange;
courtesy of William E. Doherty, Jr.,
Class of 1940. 91.023.003

This pelike—a two-handled wide-
bellied vessel usually used for wine or
water—is a good example of South
Italian pottery of the fourth century
B.C. It shows a scene where a naked
man with a fillet on his head and a
cloth draped over his arm holds an
open box (cista) and mirror. He runs
before a woman, turning back to look
at her. She wears a chiton and sandals, and carries a fan and a fillet. She
is adorned with earrings, necklace,
and bracelets. A bunch of grapes
hangs on the wall behind them, and
flowers rise from the ground below.
A bowl (phiale) lies on the ground,
and two rosettes and another fillet fill
the empty space behind the figures.
The piece may represent a couple
exchanging gifts at the time of their
wedding.

The addition of white or yellow
paint for highlights is typical of South
Italian red-figure pottery and adds to
the impression here of ornamental and
highly decorated pottery. Large palmettes under the handles complete the
decoration.

Excavated in Taranto, 1916.

NHR

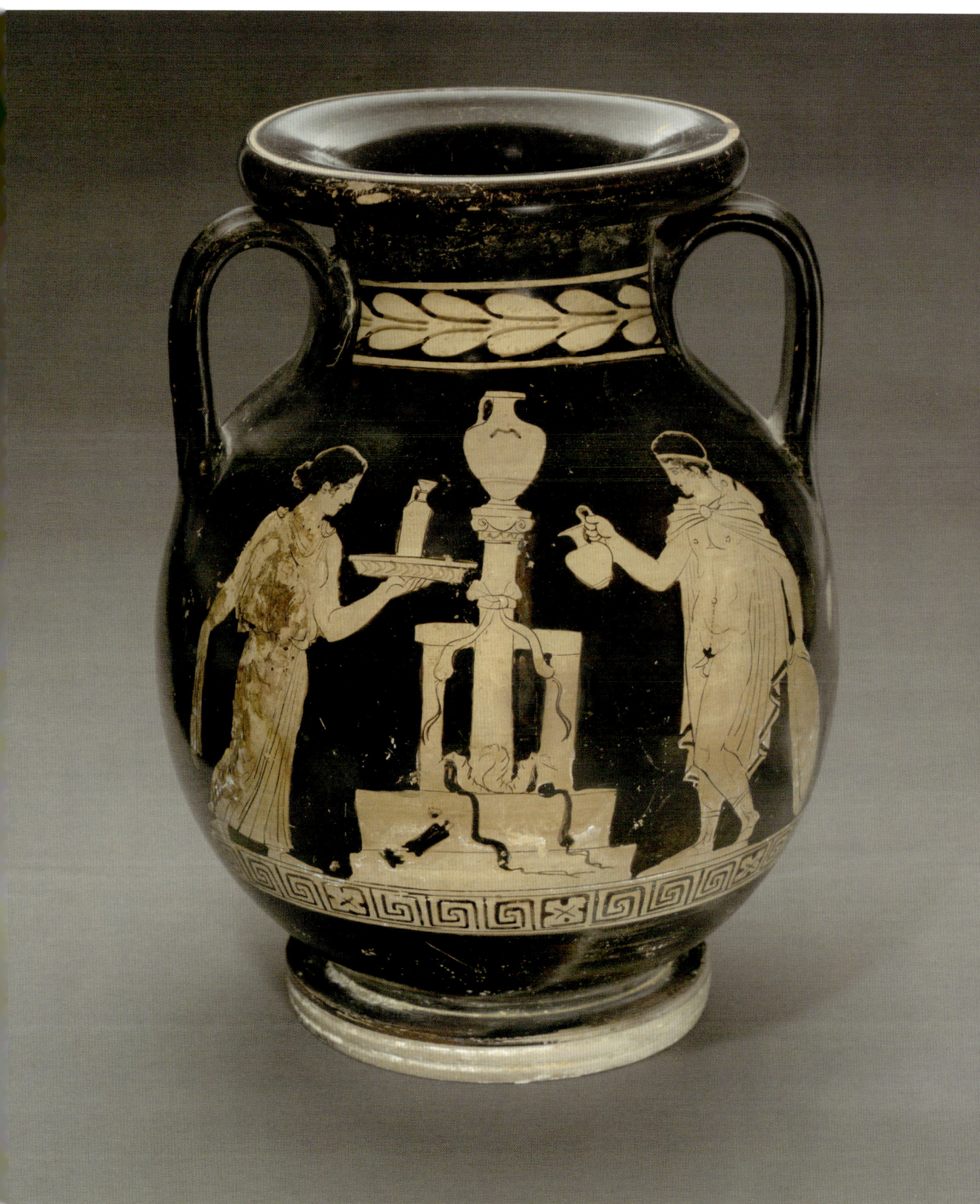

a.

7.

Red-Figure Pelike, attributed
to the Tarporley Painter or his circle
ca. 410–380 B.C.
"Electra and Orestes at the tomb of
their father Agamemnon"

Apulia

Ceramic. 31.75 x 23.50cm

Transfer from the History of Art
Collection. 74.074.007

A man and woman present offerings at a grave which is adorned with ribbons and a hydria, or water jar, on the top. The grave monument is made up of an unfluted Ionic column on two steps. The woman at left wears a chiton, slippers, and a necklace of beads, and holds a tasseled ribbon in her right hand. With her left, she presents an offering in a flat bowl or basket that has a lekythos standing in it. Note that a second lekythos, broken, lies on the steps at the foot of the altar. These pots are the same kind of vessel as our catalogue number 4, the white-ground lekythos. The man is naked save for the cloth hanging over his shoulders and clasped with a brooch. He holds a shield, and offers a libation from an olpe (a one-handled pot). This scene has been interpreted as Electra and Orestes at the grave of their father Agamemnon, and may illustrate a scene from a play by Aeschylus, *The Choephorai.*

On the back side of the pot, called Side B, a naked man, with cloth around his arm, pursues a running woman who turns back toward her pursuer. She carries a box in one hand and a ribbon in the other. The "B" side of most Greek pots is meant to be secondary in importance to the main scene on the other, or "A" side.

The relief lines that outline the reserved portions of the vase (the parts that are still reddish clay) can clearly be seen here.

PUBLISHED:
Barlow and Coleman, 1979,
p.219-225, Pl. 32.

NHR

b

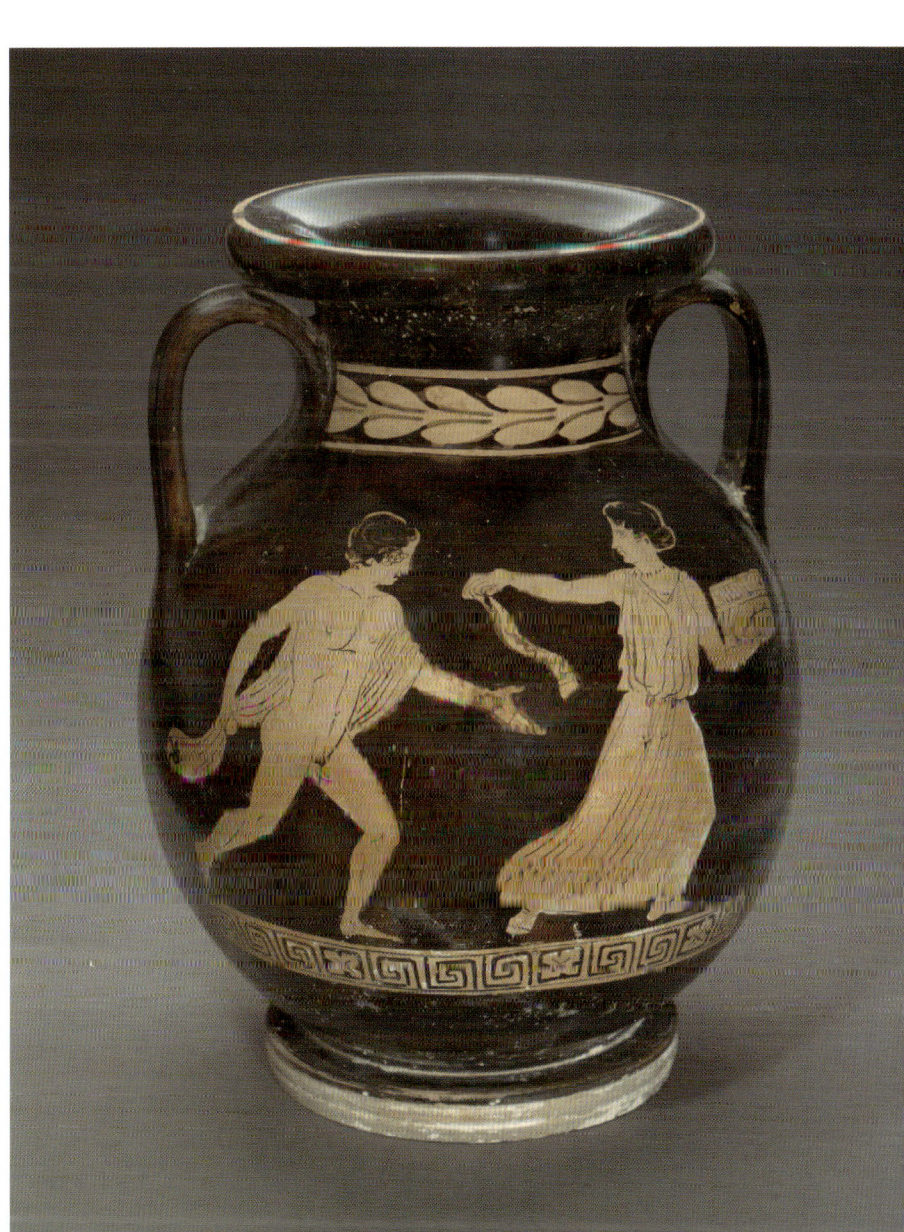

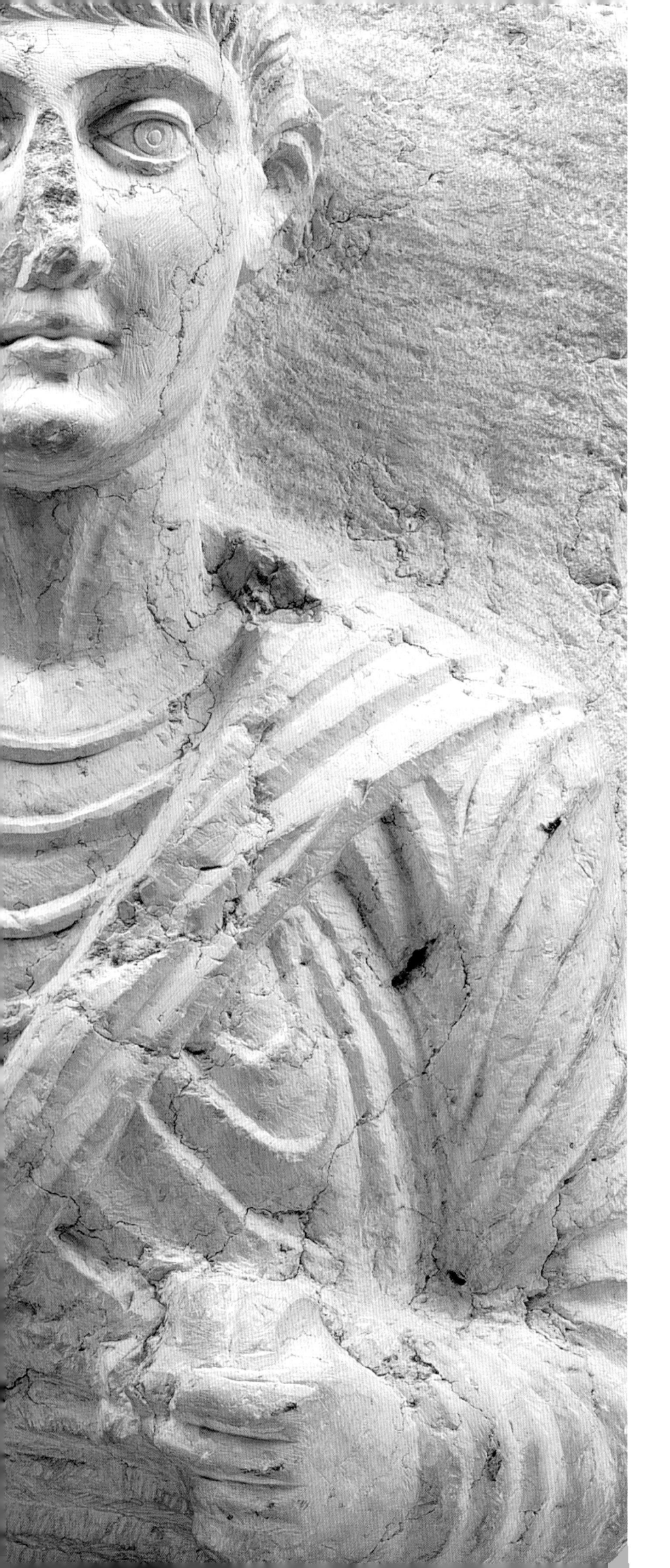

SCULPTURE

THE ETRUSCAN, GREEK, AND ROMAN sculpture in the Herbert F. Johnson Museum, as sampled in this catalogue, exhibits a number of different materials used—clay, stone, and bronze— each of which required different techniques and skills on the part of the artist. Often the choice of material was dictated by what was available in the region. The range of heads represented varies from generic to specific, and from idealized to realistic, depending on the period when something was made, as well as the purpose for which it was intended. For instance, heads that decorated architecture in Etruscan lands would invariably be generic and idealized, whereas a portrait of a Roman ruler had to be recognizable and specific to the individual. Other subjects included heads of divinities and animals. The purposes of these examples range from tomb monuments to architectural decoration to free-standing sculpture. It provides a small taste of the vast capabilities of sculptors all over the ancient world.

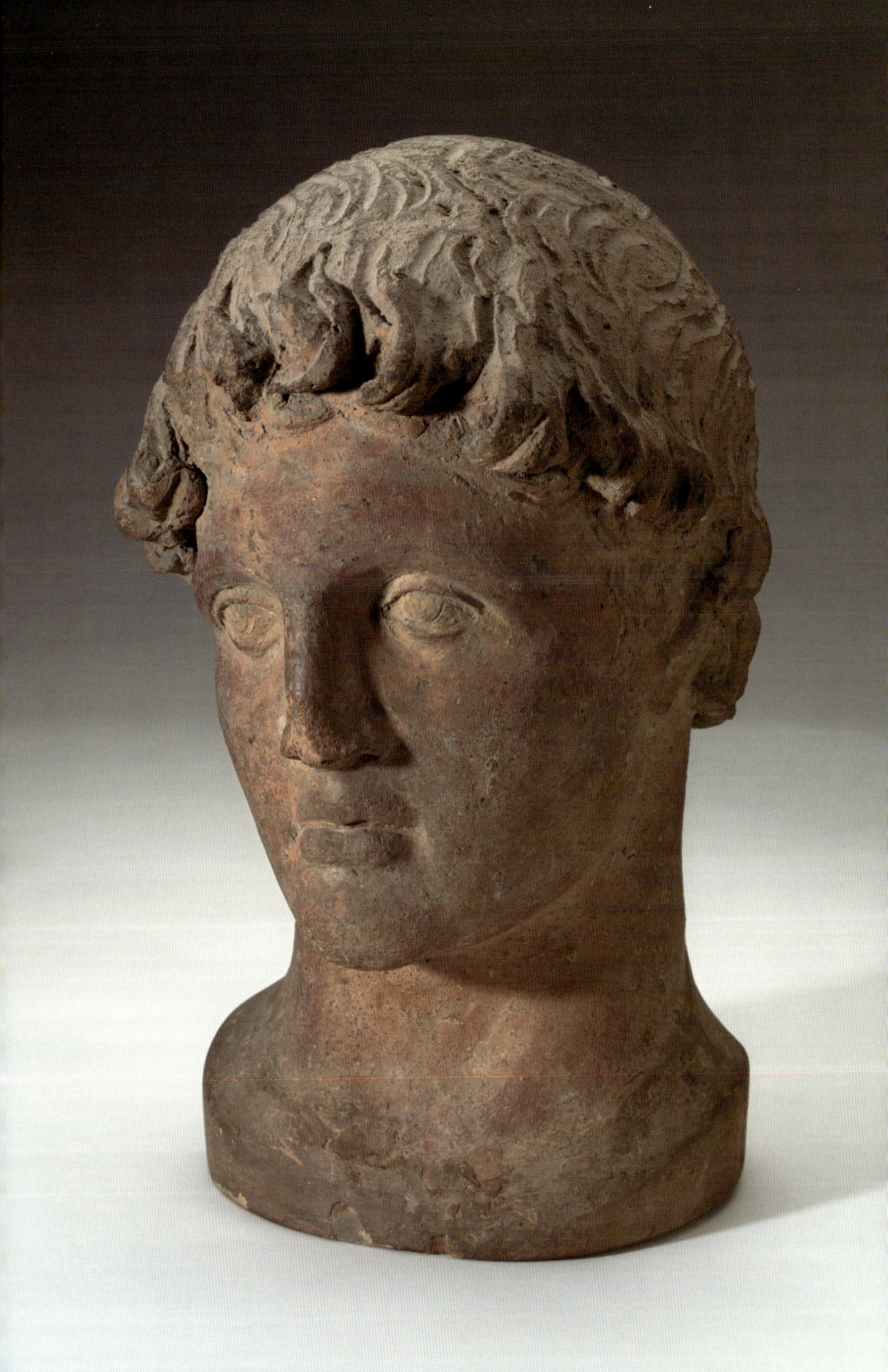

8.
Head of a Youth
Fifth century B.C.

Etruscan

Terracotta with polychrome.
Height: 29.2cm

Transfer from the History of Art
Collection. 74.074.031

The stone available to the Etruscans
was a gray, porous volcanic material,
and not particularly well suited to
sculpture. So they often turned to
clay. The easily malleable and readily
available and cheap material was
highly desirable for their purposes.

This head of a youth probably
would have been set into a whole
body, as suggested by the flanged
base at the lower neck. He has beautifully idealized, classical features
derived from Greek sculpture, but
there are also personal details, such
as the hair brushed forward on his
forehead. The tool marks defining the
strands are clearly visible, and finger
marks can be seen, too. Another
feature that adds to the interest is the
slightly turned and tipped angle of the
head. Color, now faded, was used for
hair and skin, and probably the eyes
and lips would have been highlighted
in paint. The head is hollow, as
required for terracotta sculpture;
otherwise it would have burst in the
kiln. A one-inch hole in the back of
the head was made before the piece
was fired.

NHR

9.
Head of a Woman,
Late fourth- early third century B.C.

Etruscan

Terracotta with polychrome.
Height: 25.4cm

Transfer from the History of Art
Collection. 74.074.033

Like the previous entry, this head is
made of terracotta and covered with
paint: white for hair, headpiece, and
whites of the eyes; reddish for the
skin; and black lines to highlight the
eyebrows. The irises were painted
a different color which has since
flaked off.

The head may represent a maenad,
a follower of the god Dionysus. The
smooth outline of the mantle around
her head suggests that the piece was
probably an antefix, used to decorate
the edge of a roof of a house or temple. It would have been one of many
such heads, perhaps alternating with
mules, that served as ornaments on the
roof line. It was made in a mold, and,
as in the previous piece, a hole was
left in the back for the firing process.

NHR

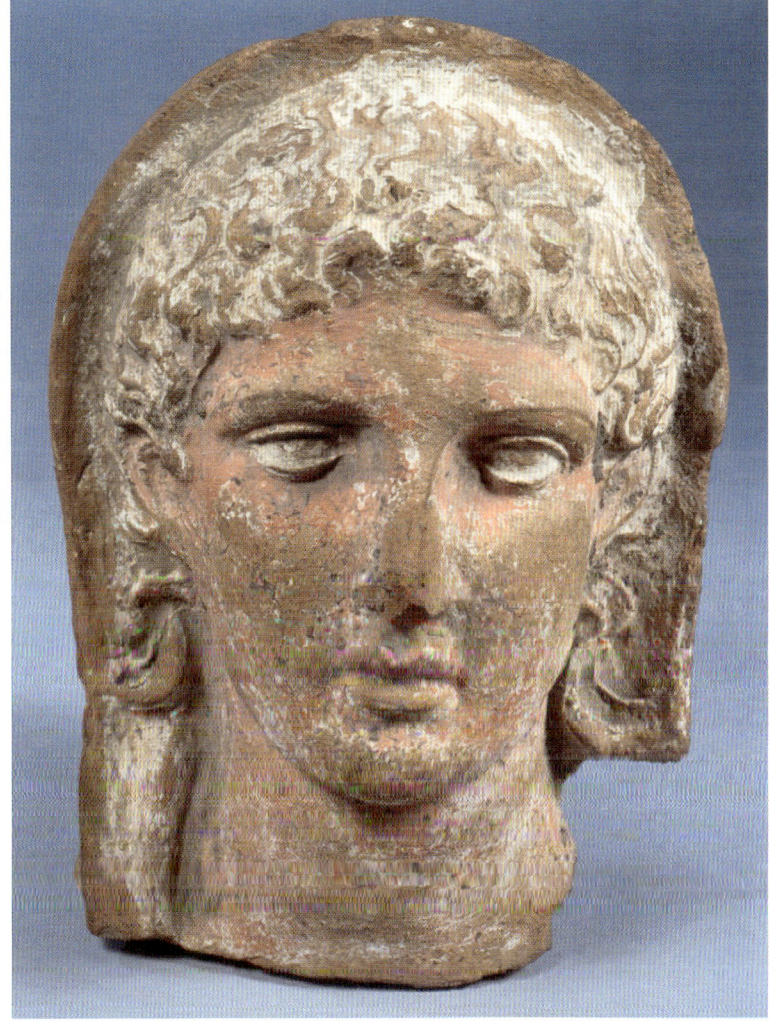

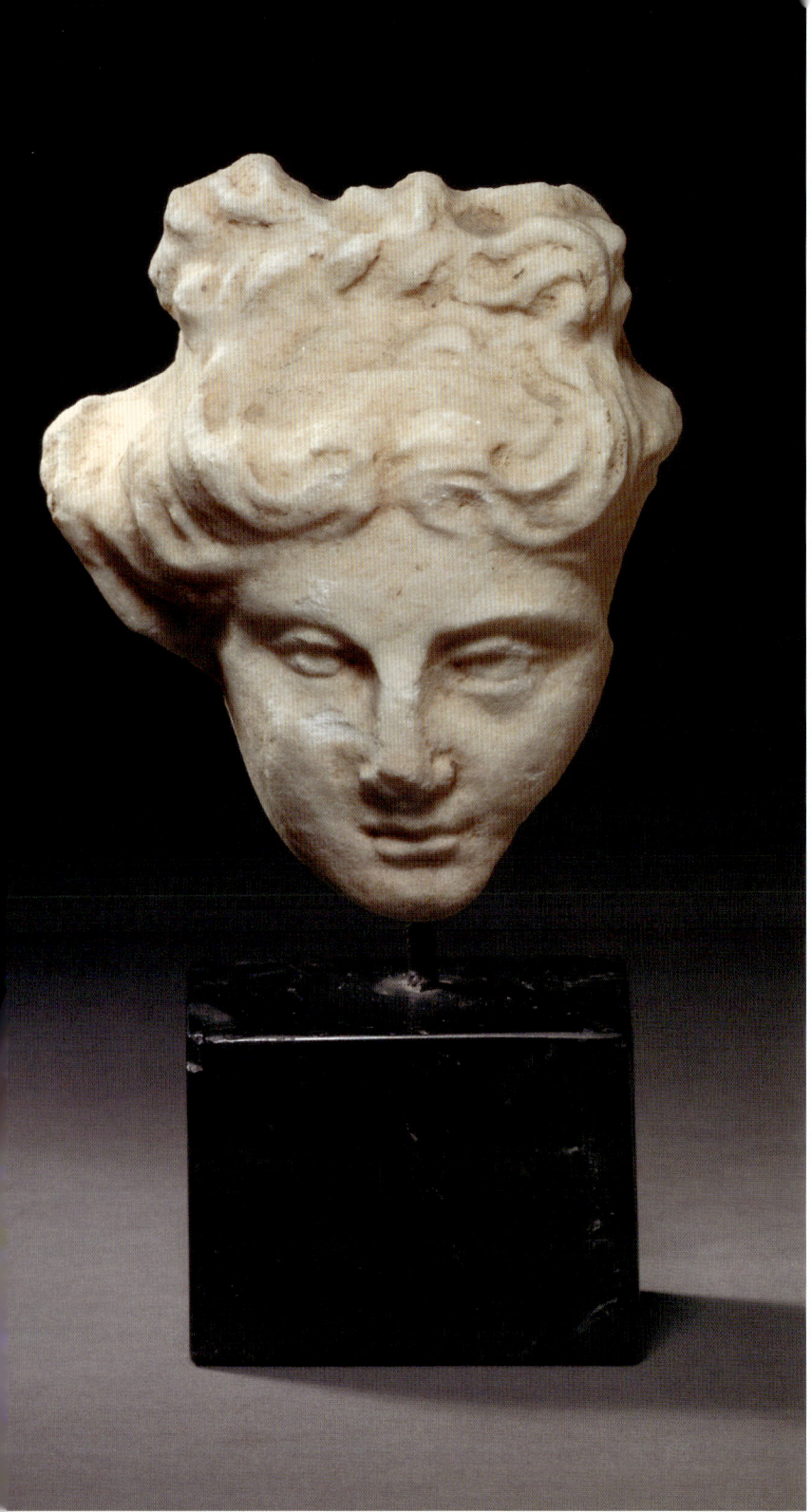

10.
Head of Apollo or Aphrodite
Late fourth- early third century B.C.

Greek

Marble. 11.4 x 9.8 x 8.3cm

Gift of Margaret and Franklin W. Robinson in memory of Celia S. R. Stillwell. 99.102

A classical face with hair parted in the center and a bow above can be either the goddess Aphrodite or the god Apollo; the fragmentary state of this small marble piece makes it impossible to be sure of the identification, although on balance it is more likely to be Aphrodite. The features—straight nose, small mouth, firm chin—are good examples of the characteristics of the idealized classical head, strong and pretty, on a small scale.

The head may have been part of a statuette gracing a private home, or it could have served as a votive offering in a shrine or temple, although such offerings were more likely to have been made of clay.

NHR

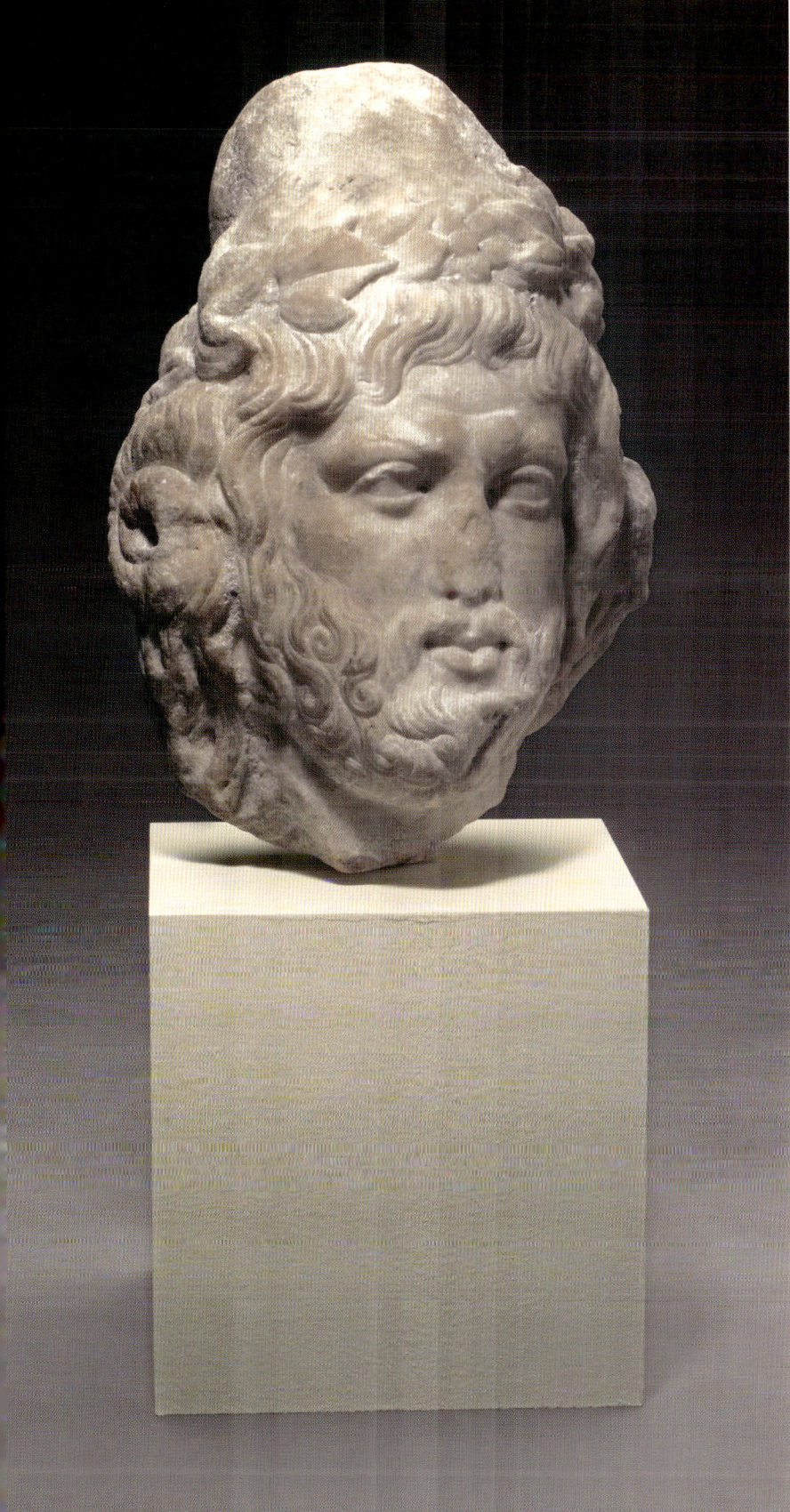

11.

Zeus Ammon

First- second century B.C.

Roman

Marble. 22.8 x 16.5 x 13.3cm

Gift of Margaret and Franklin W. Robinson. 98.100.002

Zeus (Jupiter) took many forms, and was amalgamated with local gods in lands conquered by the Romans. In this small marble sculpture, Zeus has taken on the attributes of the Egyptian god Ammon, king of the gods, the supreme creator, and god of the sun. The Greeks knew of Ammon from the seventh century B.C. onward, but the height of his popularity was reached under Alexander the Great, in the late fourth century B.C. The Romans too were continually fascinated by the amalgamation of the two gods— Jupiter and Ammon—as they were by that of several other Roman and Egyptian gods (such as Venus and Isis). The Romans not only occupied Egypt, but adopted many of its divinities whose popularity spread throughout the Roman Empire.

Zeus Ammon is identified by the ram's horns seen at the sides of his head and the cap at the top. The ram's horns also served in coins of Alexander the Great types to represent the king in the guise of Ammon (see no. 41). Zeus here also wears a garland of leaves and grapes that act like a crown below the tall cap. Typical of Zeus, he sports a beard and long hair. (Compare the Roman lamp from Syria, no. 21.) The beard has bound fully carved spirals at the end of each clump of hair.

The small size and flat surface at the back suggest that he may have been a statuette in a small shrine.

NHR

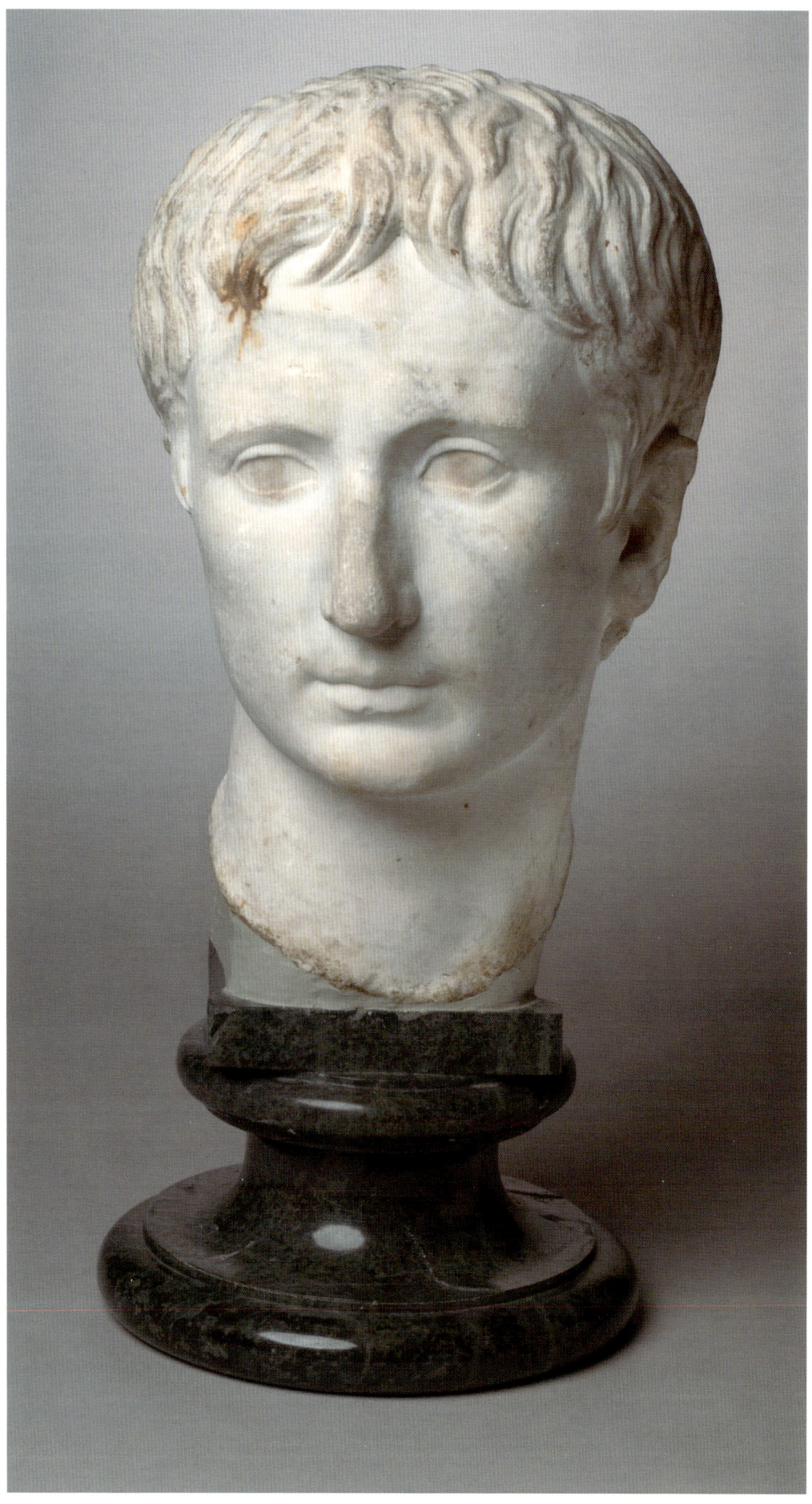

12.
Head of Augustus Caesar
ca. A.D. 30-50

Roman

Marble. Height: 54.6cm

Transfer from University Collections. 68.277

Many heads of Augustus, the first Roman emperor, have survived, but originally there must have been many more. He was a popular ruler who had a long reign, and, even after his death, sculptors carved his head over and over for countless public squares and buildings. The practice went like this: sculptors in Rome would originally carve heads of emperors that were then shipped out to the hinterlands, to be copied by distant artists who almost certainly had never seen the man himself. The head here would probably have been one of these copies made after the "Prima Porta" type. These are named for an illustrious portrait in the Vatican that shows Augustus as a full-length figure in military garb but with bare feet. (A cast of this statue is in the Sage Collection.) The piece was probably a posthumous work, showing him after he had been deified, but may have been a copy of an earlier work made during his lifetime. He was idealized even when living, but the tendency to show him as a beautiful man increased even more after his death.

In any case, the Johnson Museum head is highly idealized, and shows the handsome features of Augustus and his typical hairdo with locks of hair resting on his forehead in opposing directions. Recent cleaning and conservation have revealed coloration in the eyes to show the irises. The central part of the nose is a modern addition that has caused leaching of the adhesive upon the rest of the nose; and the right ear, which had also been repaired, is now missing. An iron stain remains on the front portion of the hair. The head was once inserted into a larger statue, as the irregular base of the neck suggests.

EXHIBITION HISTORY:
"I, Claudia: Women in Ancient Rome," Yale University Art Gallery, 9/6– 12/1/96.

PUBLISHED:
Johnson Museum, 1998, p. 99.

Kleiner and Matheson, 1996, p. 54, fig. 2.

NHR

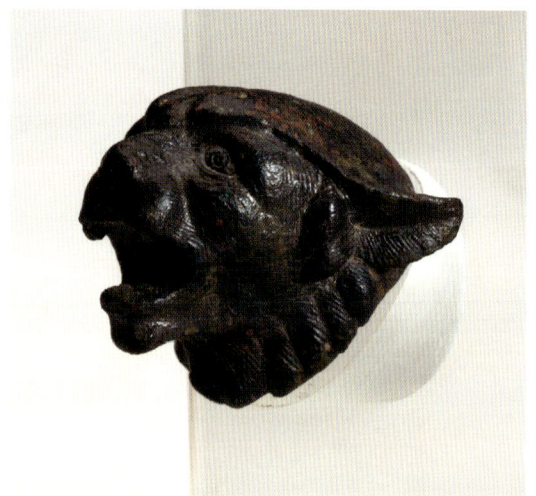

13.
Lynx's Head,
Second century A.D.

Roman
Bronze. 4.45 x 6.05 x 5.08cm

Gift of David B. Simpson, Class of 1960, and Nancy S. Simpson in memory of Leonard P. Simpson, Sp., Class of 1922

The Frank and Rosa Rhodes Collection. 95.030

The small head of a lynx may have served as a decoration for a piece of furniture, a door, or a cauldron (bronze pot). It may have had a ring through its mouth, to judge from the shape and configuration of the open mouth. Its whiskers, intense eyes, and widespread nostrils suggest a ferocious character. The incised hairs in the projecting ears, all over its face and forming the scruff under its chin attest to the fine workmanship of the modeler of this cast bronze.

Bronzes are cast hollow in a process called the lost wax technique. The sculptor models his piece in a soft material — plaster or clay — and then makes a mold in plaster, thus getting a negative of the original model. With a series of further processes, wax is used to catch all the refinements of the soft material in which the original was modeled, and these refinements will be captured in the final bronze casting which will reproduce the original exactly, but in a much more durable material. In this case, the sculptor's original details on the surface are beautifully captured in the bronze replica. He also probably added finishing details after the casting was completed.

NHR

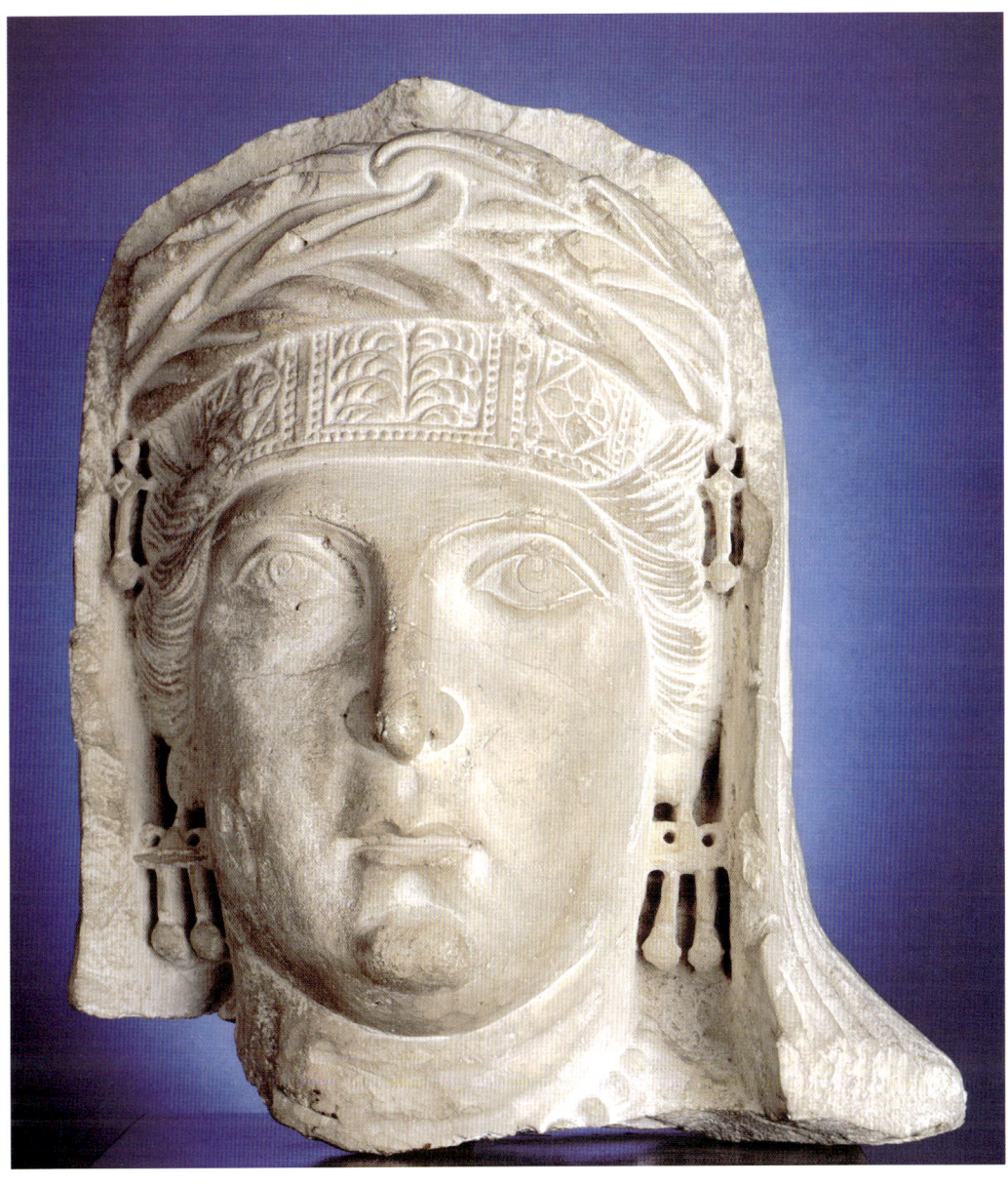

14.

Palmyrene Head

A.D. 150–200

Syria, Roman Province

Limestone. Height: 29.85cm

Transfer from University Collections,
72.021

The hard linear features of this woman's head are not meant to indicate a portrait but rather provide a generic representation of a Palmyrene woman, that is, a Roman woman from the flourishing town of Palmyra in Syria. Palmyra was on the major trade road that connected Parthia and inland Syria with the Mediterranean coast, and served as an important stop along the caravan route. Riches from the east were brought to the Roman world along the road, making Palmyra one of the important cities that prospered due to this flourishing trade. The head was used for a grave monument that would have included numerous other graves and funerary heads within a large burial chamber located beyond the city walls (see fig. 8). Such chambers normally would be lined with rows of tomb reliefs like the Johnson head, but showing the figure down to the waist, with both hands in a traditional position (one arm tucked under a robe). Our piece, too, must have looked like that.

The head is decorated with an elaborate headband, strands of hair, and a cloth with many folds. The woman also wears earrings and bangles, all of which were deeply drilled. These features are typical of Palmyrene heads, which favored lots of decorative linear details, both for men and women, but little expression on the face.

Palmyrene sculpture has distinctive features that on the whole are not typical of Roman art, but reflect instead a Near Eastern tradition that had developed in this region over two millennia. These characteristics included a love of decorative details, linear patterns, and frontality. The Roman talent for showing individualism and character in portraits is more or less lost in the sculpture of this provincial region, but instead, far more attention is paid to patterns of drapery, jewelry, and other ornate features. Palmyra serves as a kind of meeting ground between the Graeco-Roman traditions of the west and the Near Eastern features of the east.

NHR

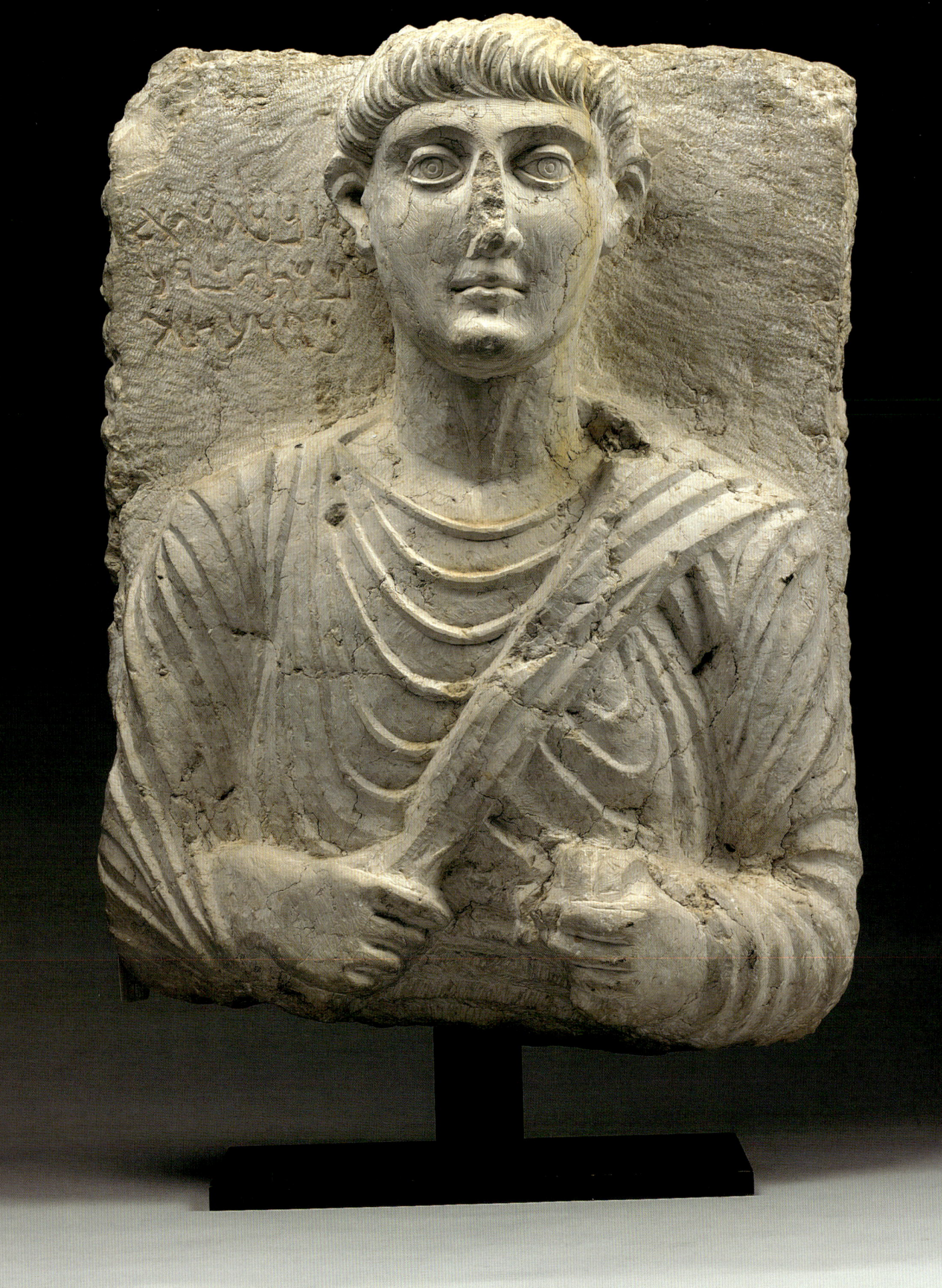

15.

Palmyrene Bust

Second– third century A.D.

"Gadia's funerary monument"

Syria, Roman Province

Limestone. 55 x 44 cm.

Gift of Genevieve and Richard Tucker, Class of 1950. 2002.21

Our second example of a Palmyrene funerary relief is preserved in the form of the complete stone that would have been set in the tomb wall, as shown in the picture of the Tomb of Yarkai in the Damascus Museum. A young man wearing a robe (himation) stares out frontally toward the viewer, in the manner typical of Palmyrene reliefs. The pupils and irises are incised with prominent lines that add to the sense of staring. In later Roman sculpture, the incision of the eyes substitutes for the color that has been added to show the details of the eye in earlier times, as seen on the head of Augustus (no. 12). With his right hand the man holds a branch, probably a palm, as is often seen on tomb reliefs of male figures. In his left hand he holds a piece of cloth, probably a loop of his own drapery. Once again, the features are not strictly those of a portrait, although the rounded line of his chin and bangs on his forehead may be features specific to this individual.

An Aramaic inscription on the relief, beside his head, says: "Woe! Gadiâ (son of) Taibbol, (son of) Nur_teh."

The artist has used the patterns of the robe and undergarment to make a lively play of linear designs. The sharp ridges of the cloth contrast strikingly with the flat surface of his hands. The face, on the other hand, has a charming roundness to it, emphasized by the projecting ears and the full head of patterned hair. The marks of a toothed chisel are clearly visible all over the flat limestone slab.

PROVENANCE:

Èmile-Pierre Bertone, Paris, late nineteenth century; sold at Hôtel des Ventes de Neuilly-sur-Seine, Dec. 14, 1931, no. 681.

Bertone (1867–1931) was an architect who worked at Palmyra in 1897.

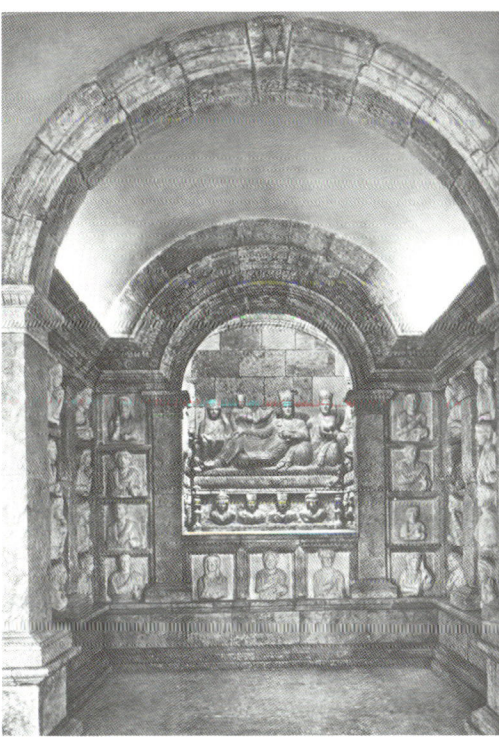

Fig. 8:

Tomb of Yarkai (A.D. 175–200), Palmyra. National Museum of Damascus.

PUBLISHED:

Jean-Baptiste Chabot, *Journal Asiatique*, 9ème série, vol. 10, 1897, no. 52, and 1898, II, p. 287

Charles Clermont-Ganneau, *Recueil d'archéologie orientale*, vol. 5, Paris, 1902, p. 41

Mark Lidzbarski, *Ephemeris für semitische Epigraphik*, vol. I, Giessen, 1902, p. 347

Répertoire d'épigraphie sémitique, I, 1905, p. 216, no. 266

CIS (Corpus Inscriptionum Semiticarum) II, section 3, part 2 (text=1947; plates=1954), pp. 446f., no. 4529, pl. 46

Delbert R. Hillers and Eleonora Cussini, *Palmyrene Aramaic Texts*, Baltimore, 1995, p. 146, no. PAT. 0890

NHR

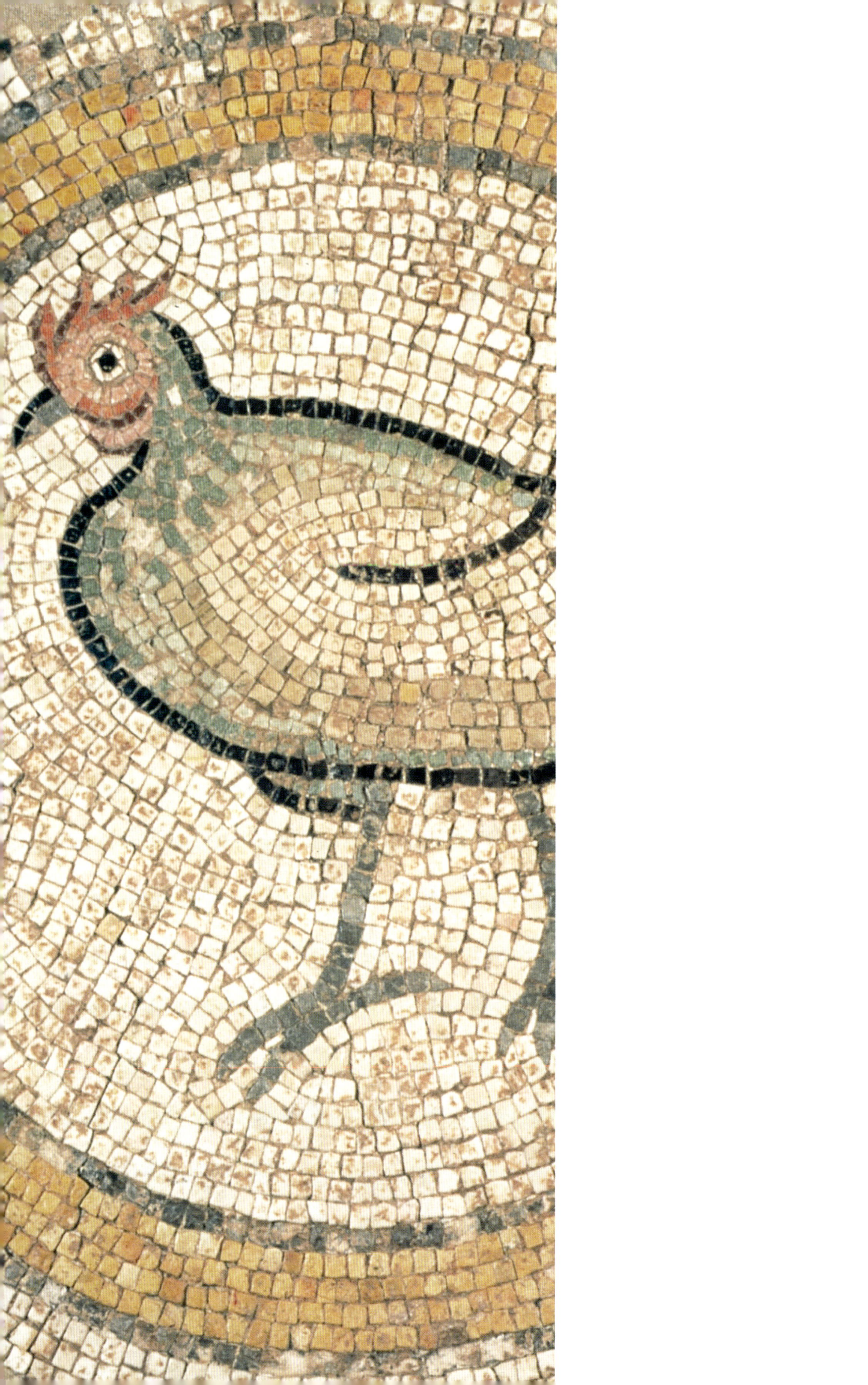

LIFE AND DEATH
IN ANTIQUITY

OBJECTS FROM DAILY LIFE often tell us a great deal about the people who used them to promote their religious beliefs, help them with the requirements of everyday living, or provide comfort at the ceremonies associated with death. Such items include votive offerings to the gods, funerary objects, or architectural decoration. From a single everyday object, such as an ordinary lamp, we can learn about how Romans lit their way at night using common oil, while at the same time learn about their religious imagery. Funerary objects often reflect the rituals of a particular time and place. Practices initiated by the Etruscans in the sixth century B.C. evolved over time and influenced the practices of the Romans several hundred years later, as seen both in rituals and in the contents of tombs.

We sample a few objects here, often humble ones, to give a sense of the kinds of things that have been found in homes or tombs that are so revealing of the ancient people they served.

Clay Figurines

Many of the clay figurines found from early Greek times were votive offerings intended to serve some purpose in people's lives. The donor would present the item to a god in a shrine or temple, incanting his wish at the same time. Usually the image portrayed would relate closely to what was wished for by the person making the offering, and the idea was that one would give something to the gods, with the understanding that the gods would then give back something in return. These items were common, and were never meant to be "works of art," although today we admire them for their simplicity, charm, and directness. The following two figurines from the Late Geometric period are the kinds of objects that people would typically have offered to the gods when wishing for success in a race or for foals from their fillies; or they could have been toys for a child. The two pieces below could have been made in Athens or Boeotia where the same tradition took hold.

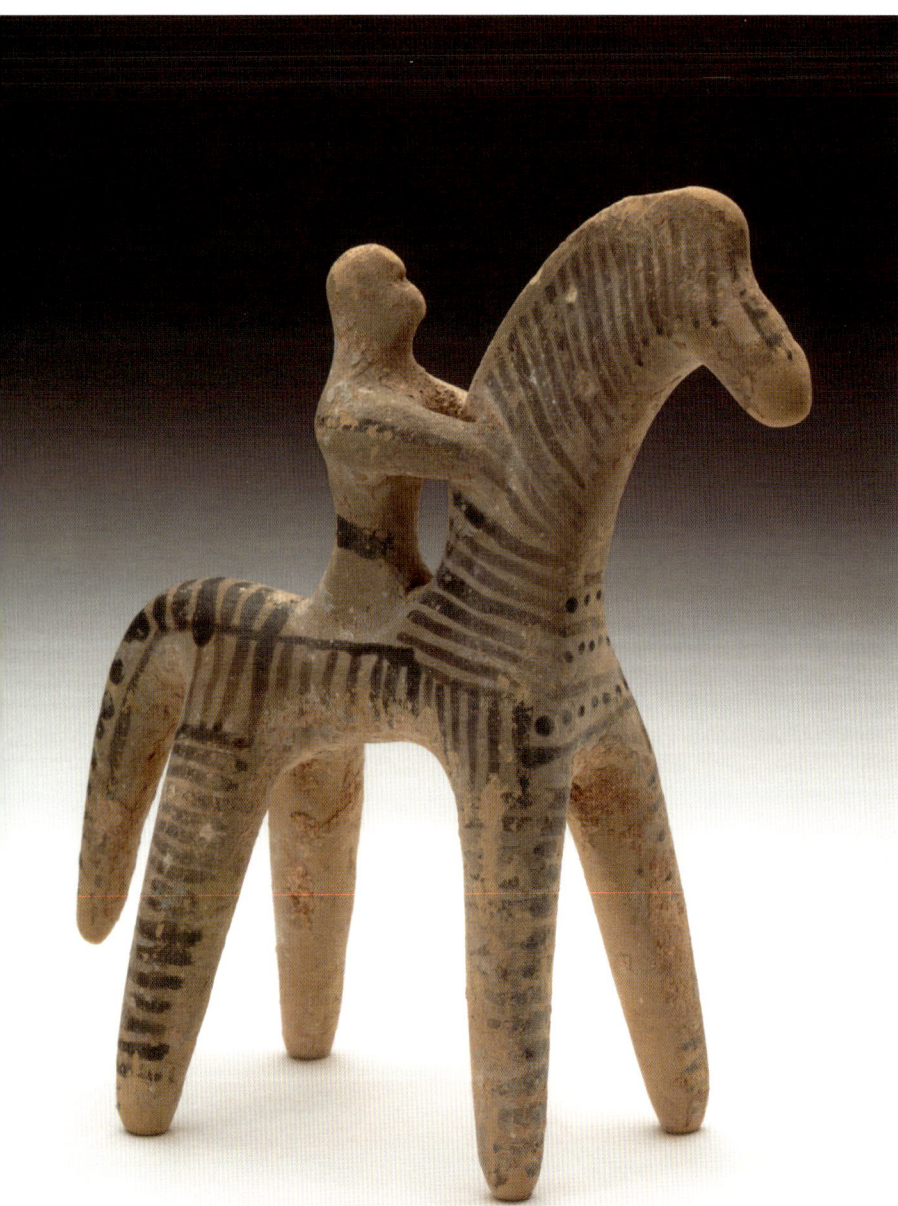

16.
Horse and Rider
ca. 700 B.C.

Athens or Boeotia

Terracotta. 12.7 x 11.43cm

Gift of Norbert Schimmel. 54.079

Geometric artists concentrated on basic forms and simple geometric designs. Here it is perfectly clear that the subject is a man on a horse, even though the man's legs are not shown. His arms grasp the mane and neck of the horse, or perhaps he is intended to be holding reins. He is wearing a belt. The horse is covered with parallel lines and dots that help to define the body parts, such as mane or tail, by changes in direction of the lines; and they also provide attractive decoration. Note that details of faces, either on man or on horse, seem not to have been important to the maker of this terracotta.

NHR

17.
Geometric Horses
Seventh century B.C.

Athens or Boeotia

Terracotta. 14 x 10.8cm

Bequest of J.M. Hanson,
Class of 1951. 51. 63.429

This statuette probably represents two horses rather than one horse with two heads. The two heads emerging from one body indicate that the horses are parallel and walking together. The animal legs are considerably shorter than on the previous terracotta. Here, the decoration consists of widely-spaced parallel lines and diamonds (or lozenges) on the chest. The black glaze on the thinning parts of the necks effectively suggests manes. The whole piece had first been covered with a dark brown slip, over which the black glaze was then applied.

NHR

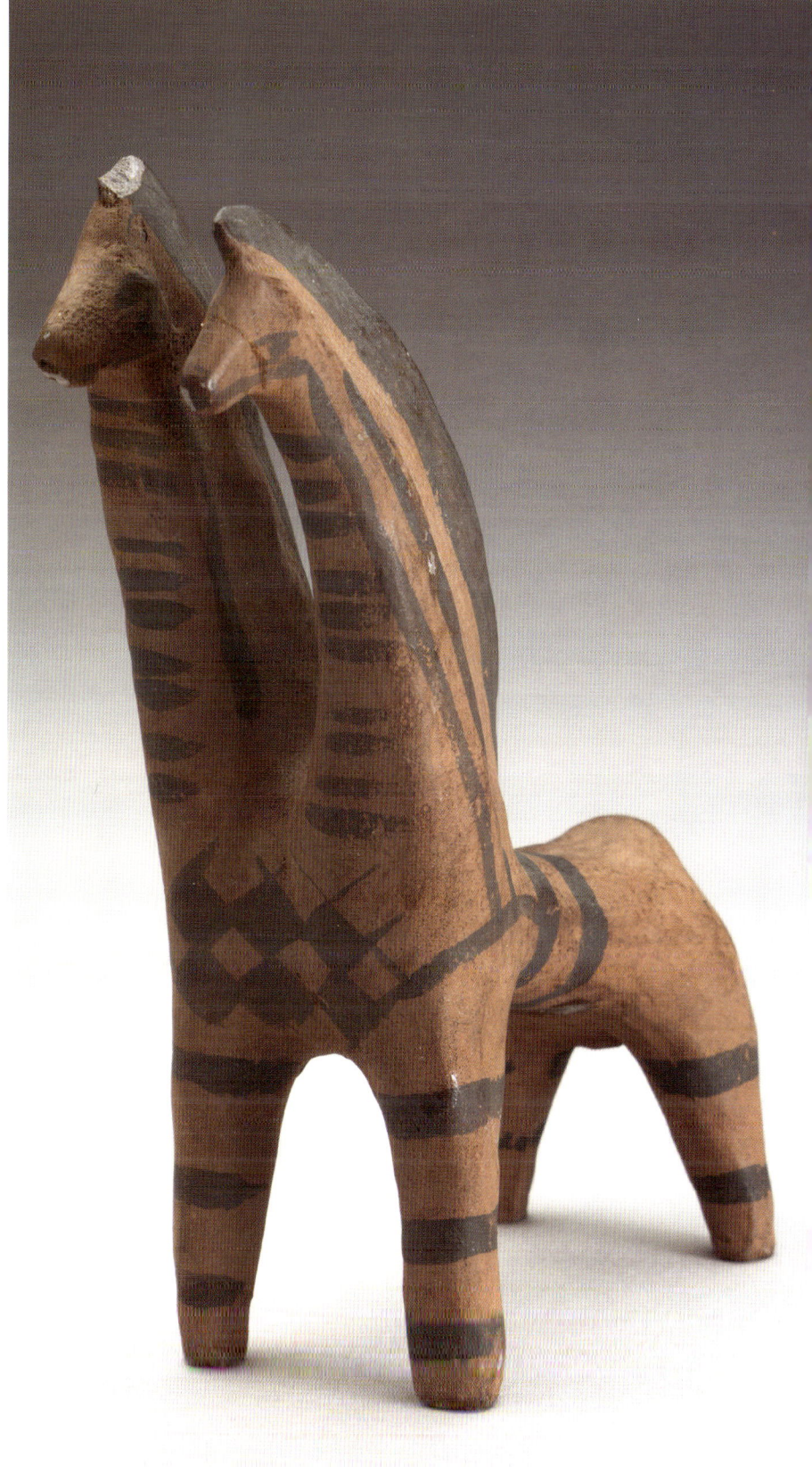

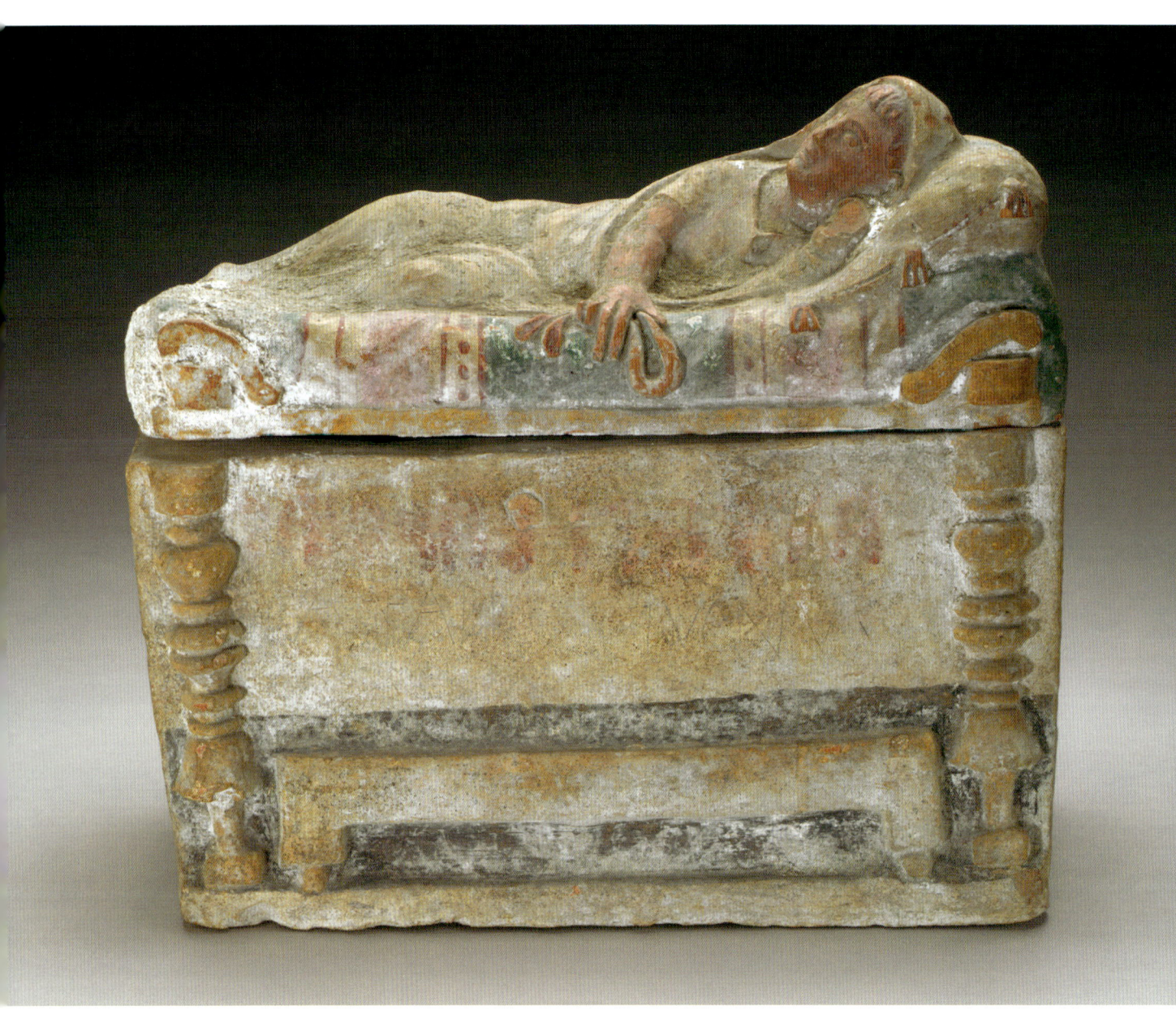

18.
Cinerary Urn
Fourth or third century B.C.

Etruria

Terracotta with polychrome.
27.9 x 32.4 x 16.2cm

Transfer from University Collections.
74.074.009

The lid represents a man holding a red ribbon, or fillet, in his hand as he lies on a mattress, supported by a pillow with red tassels. The man himself looks upward as he lies comfortably on the bed, dressed in a long white toga. The lower part of the urn depicts the legs of the bed he rests on, and the footstool that lies underneath. This is a late example of a long tradition in Etruscan practice, where in earlier centuries a body would be placed in a sarcophagus (coffin) within a tomb; instead, in later periods, the ashes of a cremated body would be placed in an urn. In both practices, using either the sarcophagus or the cinerary urn, it was customary to depict the dead person, a man or woman, lying on a bed.

At the head and foot of the mattress, curved decorative elements serve as the fulcra—typical ornaments found on ancient beds. The upper body of the man here is quite three-dimensional, but the lower body is much flatter. The gaily painted mattress has pink and dark red paint, alternating with green. There was also painted decoration below the footstool.

Illegible letters are painted across the front, and an Etruscan inscription, possibly providing the deceased's name, A VAPII LUCNUL, was scratched into the clay (after firing) as well. The inscription reads left to right, indicating a later rather than an earlier date. The only occurrences of those names are at Chiusi, suggesting that this was likely the provenance of our piece. A Latin version of the inscription might read something like A. Fabius Lucinius, but this is really speculation.

EXHIBITION HISTORY:
"Vessels: Stylistic and Functional Reflections of the Ancient World," University Art Gallery, SUNY, Binghamton, 10/20–11/19/78.

NHR & PIK

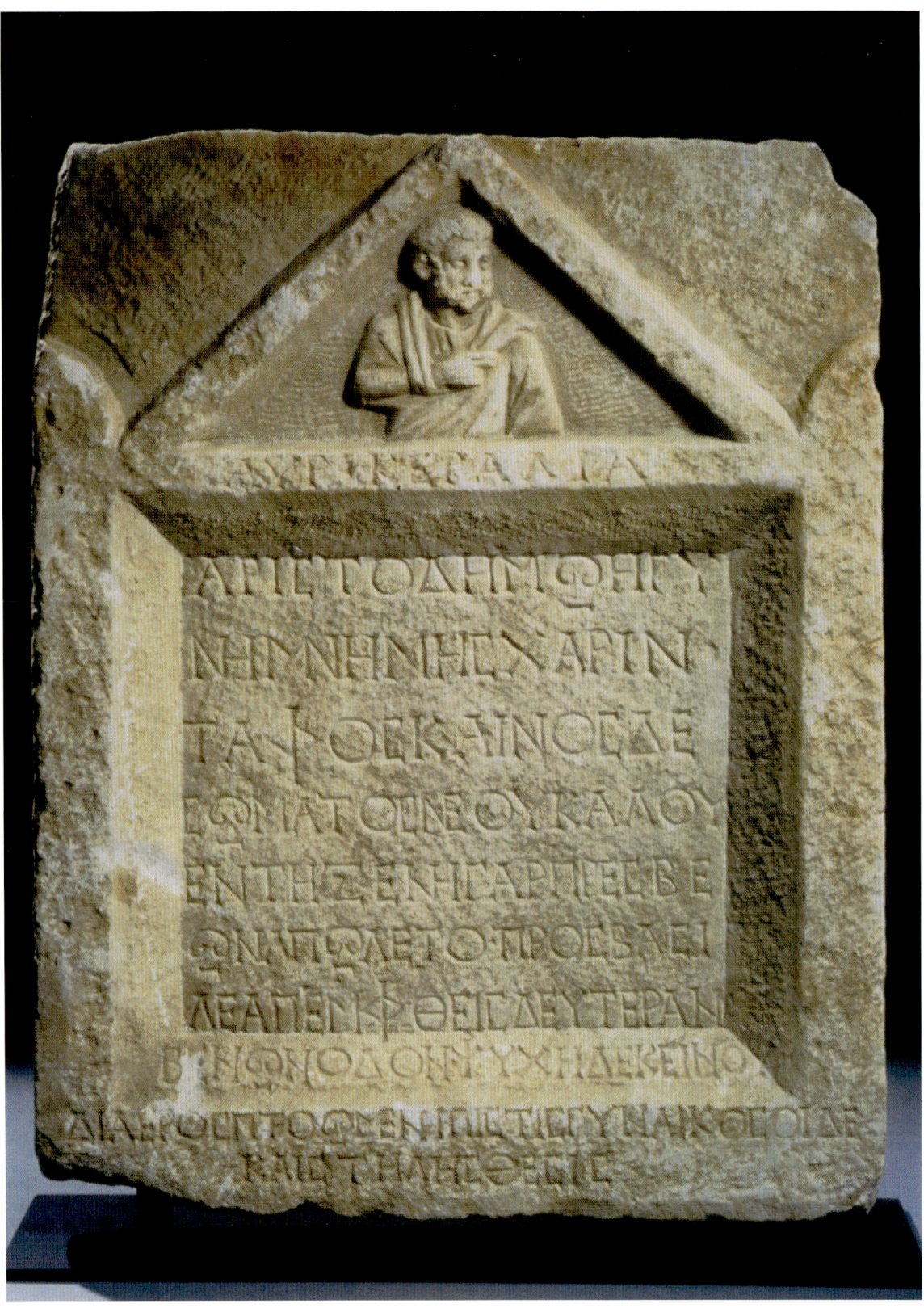

19.
Stele
Third century A.D.
"Aristodemus's funerary monument"

Asia Minor

Marble. 61 x 49.5 x 5.1cm

David M. Solinger, Class of 1926
Fund. 94.053

The honoree wearing his pallium (heavy cloak) looks out sideways from the pediment of this slab of marble, which is inscribed as follows:

ΑΥΡ ΚΕΡΑΛΙΑ
ΑΡΙΣΤΟΔΗΜΩ Η ΓΥ
ΝΗ ΜΝΗΜΗΣ ΧΑΡΙΝ
ΤΑΦΟΣ ΚΑΙΝΟΣ ΔΕ
ΣΩΜΑΤΟΣ ΝΕΟΥ ΚΑΛΟΥ
ΕΝ ΤΗ ΞΕΝΗ ΓΛΡ ΠΡΕΣΒΕ
ΩΝ ΑΠΩΛΕΤΟ ΠΡΟΣ ΒΑΣΙ
ΛΕΑ ΠΕΜΦΘΕΙΣ ΔΕΥΤΕΡΑΝ
ΒΕΝΩΝ ΟΔΟΝ ΨΥΧΗ Δ ΕΚΕΙΝΟΥ
ΔΙ ΑΕΡΟΣ ΠΤΟΩΜΕΝΗ ΠΙΣΤΙΣ
ΓΥΝΑΙΚΟΣ ΟΙΔΕ
ΚΑΙ ΣΤΗΛΗΣ ΘΕΣΙΣ*

Αυρ Κεραλία
Ἀριστοδημω ἡ γυ-
νη μνήμης χάριν
ταφος καινος δε
σωματος νεόυ καλου
ἐν τη ξενη γαρ πρεσββε-
ων ἀπωλετο προς βασι-
λεα πεμφθεις δευτέραν
βένων *(sic)* ὁδόν ψυχη δ᾽ ἐκείνου
δι᾽ ἀέρος π⟨οτ⟩ωμένη πίστις γυναικος ⟨ω⟩δε
και στήλης θέσις.*

TRANSLATION:
Aurelia Ceralia erected this memorial to her husband Aristodemus
An empty tomb for his fair young body.
For in a foreign land, while on an embassy to the emperor and
Travelling a road for the second time, he perished.
To his soul, as it soars through the air,
The loyalty of his wife and this tombstone are dedicated.

The inscription, written in iambic verse (excluding line 1), indicates that Aristodemus' wife, Aurelia Ceralia, had this grave monument carved for her husband who died in a faraway land and thus could not be brought back for burial at home.

The artist did not have enough space and therefore had to go onto the borders to conclude his inscription. He miscalculated once again, as seen by the fact that the letters near the bottom get smaller and smaller so that the carver could fit in everything. The piece is interesting too because the tool marks are still visible.

Such grave monuments could be found all over the Roman Empire, often with formulaic inscribed texts that were repeated over and over. This particular inscription, though, has the ring of specific circumstances. One did not have to be particularly wealthy to merit this kind of tombstone, although as an ambassador to the Roman emperor, Aristodemus would have most likely been a fairly wealthy and distinguished citizen of his city. Even ordinary people could usually afford to mark the graves of their relatives with an inscribed stone, which would be placed in a cemetery that typically lined the streets outside the walls of a Roman town.

Published: Petzl, Georg. "Inschriften aus Phrygien," *Epigraphica Anatolica*. Vol. 31 (1999), p. 95-97

* There are odd variations of spelling in Lines 4 and 9, with the words ΚΑΙΝΟΣ (ΚΕΝΟΣ) and ΒΕΝΩΝ (ΒΛΙΝΩΝ) respectively. There are also two misspellings in Line 10: ΠΤΟΩΜΕΝΗ, which should read ΠΟΤΩΜΕΝΗ, and ΟΙΔΕ, which should be ΩΔΕ.

Thanks to Kevin Clinton for help with the inscription.

NHR

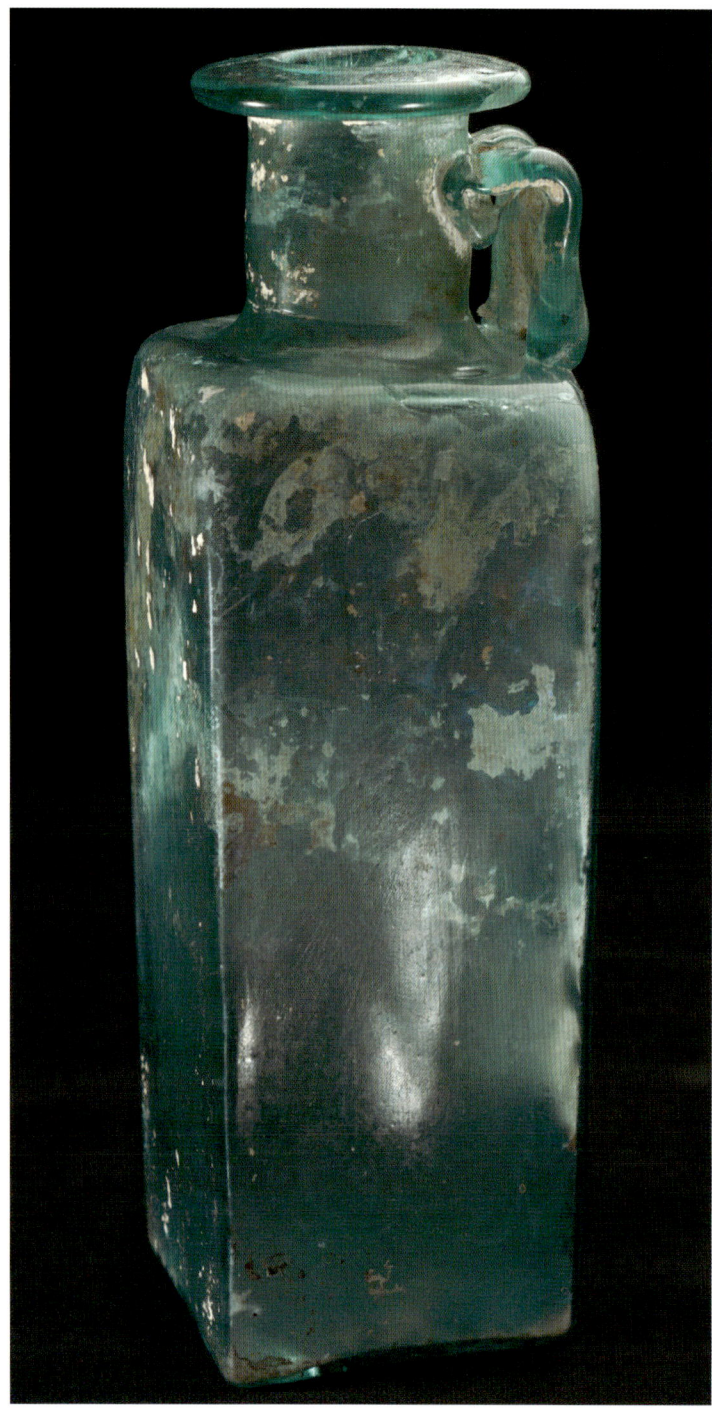

20.
Bottle
First or second century A.D..

Roman

Glass. 31.5 x 10 x 9.5cm.
Neck ext.: 5.5 cm; int.:3.9 cm

Promised gift of the Wunsch Foundation

This square bottle was blown into a mold, and the wide handle, made up of two distinct elements fused together, was welded to the neck and shoulder while softened by the heat. The base of the bottle has a pattern of four convex concentric rings in relief around a central boss surrounded by right angle patterns at each corner of the square outline. A mold of this design is reported from the city of Cologne in Germany.

This type of bottle has been found in Pompeii and Herculaneum and might well have formed part of a set, as the square molded shape is easier to pack and carry around than free-blown shapes. Such a set has been found at Herculaneum. In the absence of an inscription or knowledge of the archaeological context, we cannot be very precise about the dating. The greenish color is quite standard because it was very unusual to find the pure ingredients to produce colorless glass; the slight iridescence on the surface is caused by the corrosion of the glass over the years.

AR

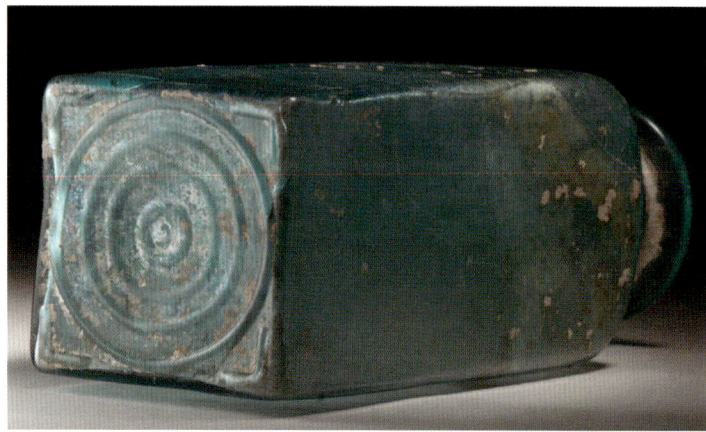

21.
Oil Lamp with Crescent Handle
ca. A.D. 100

Syria, Roman Province

Terracotta. 12.3 x 10.1 x 23.5cm

Transfer from History of Art
Collection. 74.074.035

Lamps like this show that even in
mundane and useful objects, religion
plays its role. Jupiter and his symbol,
the eagle, decorate this large terracotta
oil lamp. The god's bearded head,
with a thick head of hair, appears to
rise up from the back of a flying
eagle. A second eagle, with wings
well positioned to fit the space of the
crescent-shaped handle, completes the
references to the god.

    The lamp was clearly used in
antiquity, as can be seen by the black-
ened hole where the burning wick pro-
jected. The oil, usually olive oil,
would have been poured into this hole
for refilling as necessary. A second
smaller hole on the top served as the
vent that supplied oxygen to make the
wick burn properly. The piece was
made in a mold, and would have been
mass-produced. Thus, there would
have been many identical lamps to
this one.

NHR

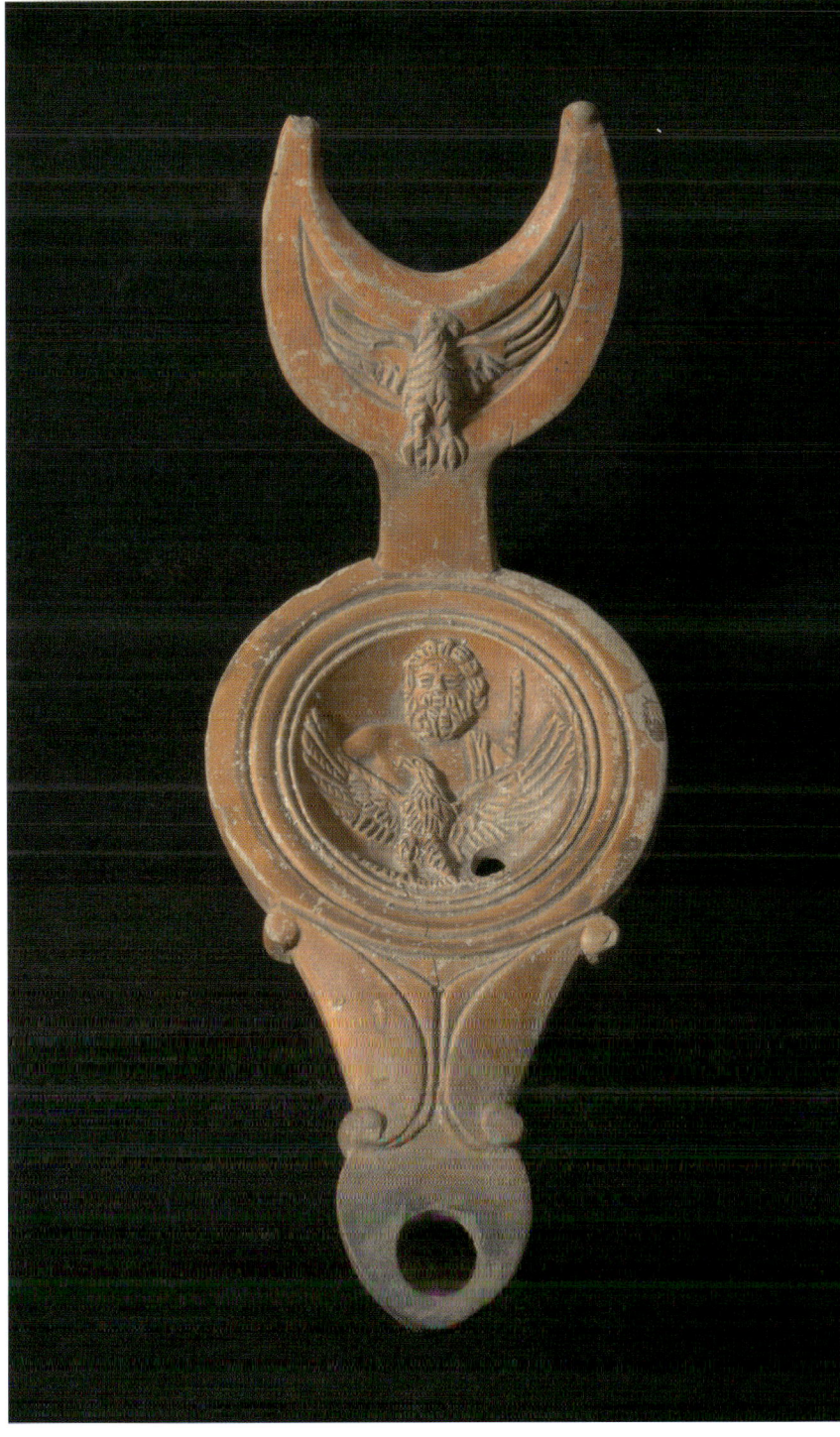

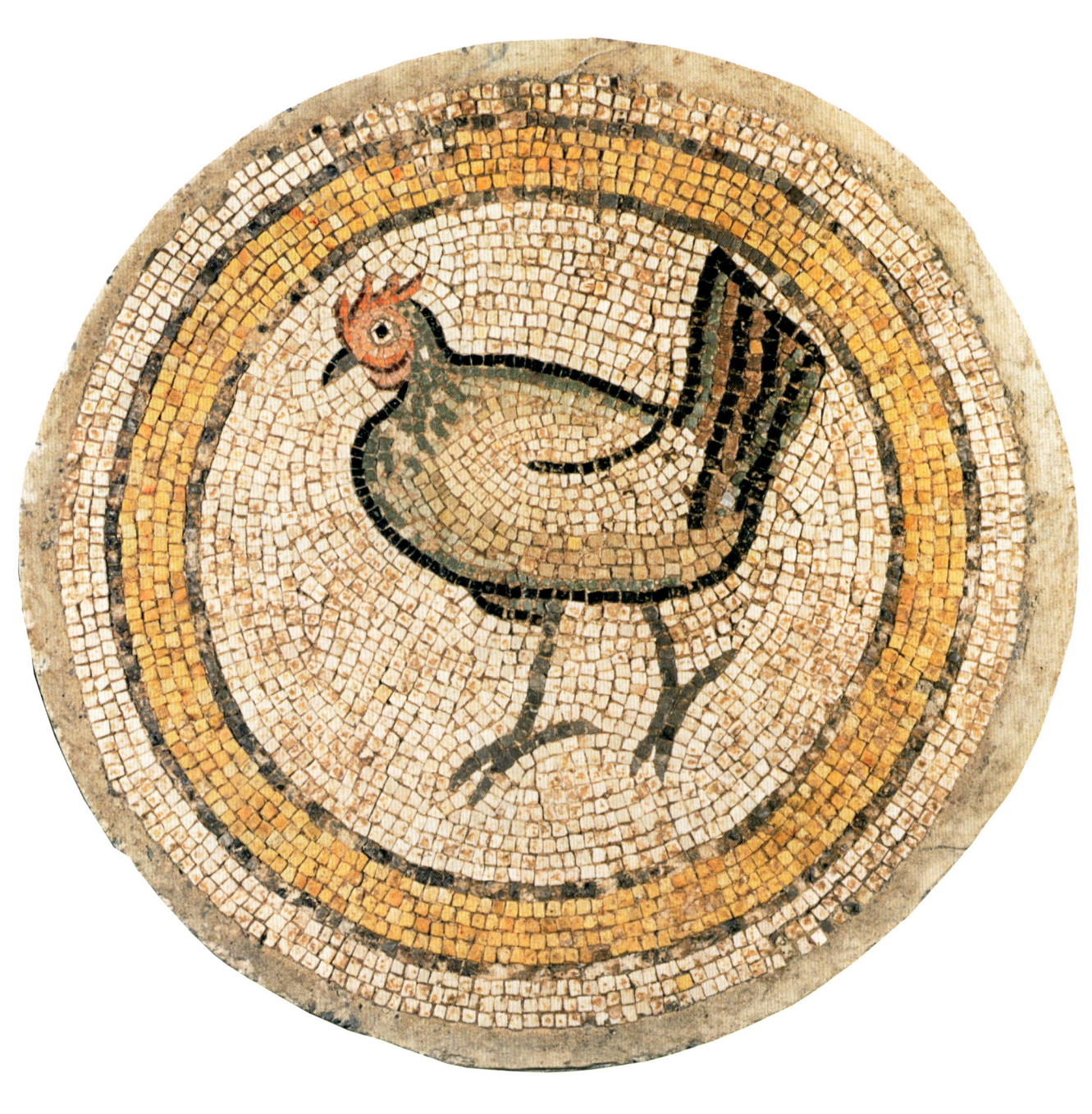

22.
Mosaic depicting a Rooster
A.D. 450-550

Syria, Roman Province

Marble tesserae. Diameter: 80.3cm

Gift of Professor and
Mrs. Meyer H. Abrams. 80.110

Early churches in Syria, as in many other places, were covered with mosaics, both on floors and walls. This fragment from a much larger mosaic, perhaps with a series of animated circles, depicts a lively rooster with tail lifted. Cocks in Christian iconography symbolize watchfulness because of their early morning crowing.

The bird's red comb and face are contrasted with grays, greens, black, and white tesserae— the square colored stones set in lime mortar to make the design. The white tesserae surrounding the bird follow its shape, while those farther from the bird simply follow the curve of the border. The mosaic probably was made from the center out, moving from the bird to the spaces around him, to the wider circles of the background.

Brightly decorated floors such as these derive from a similar practice in Roman houses, where the more elegant would have been decorated with figural mosaics that served as floor decorations, rather like carpets spread throughout the house. It was common for such mosaics to be ori-ented toward the front of a room so that as one entered, the mosaic scenes would face toward the viewer. The subject matter of Roman mosaics would also vary depending on the kind of room being decorated, such as bedroom or dining room. This practice evolved easily into imagery that was suitable for early Christian churches, and in fact often the same subjects that had served the Romans (cupids, grapevines, peacocks) would work well for the new Christian patrons. The influence of Roman mosaics continued into the Middle Ages and beyond.

NHR

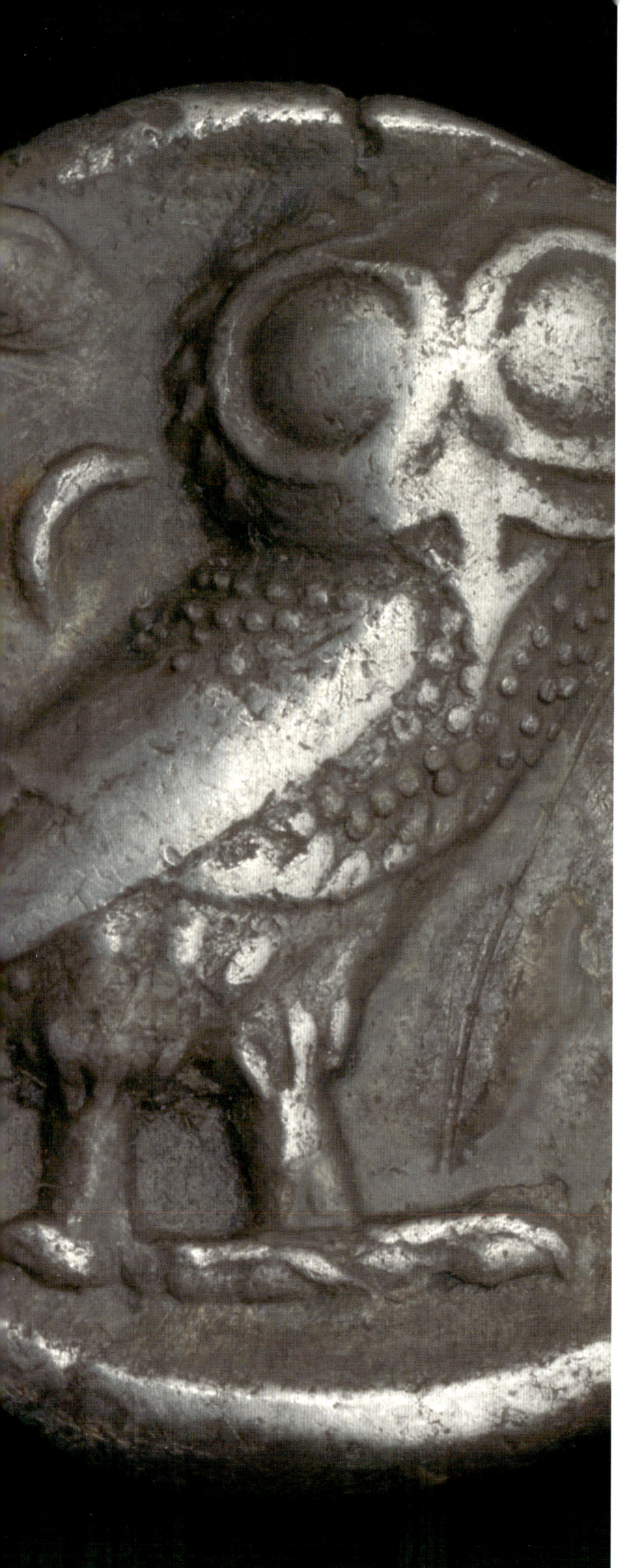

COINS

COINS OF THE GREEK WORLD

The Earliest Coinage

Trade in the Mediterranean had existed for millennia without coinage, but in the seventh century B.C. a remarkable invention took place in western Asia Minor, the effects of which are still with us today. The Lydians were said to be the first people to strike coins in the region (seventh century B.C., with opinion divided on a starting-date between ca. 650 and 615), and in the beginning they used electrum, a natural alloy of gold and silver that occurred in the neighborhood of Sardis. Later on, probably in the reign of King Croesus (whence the expression "rich as Croesus"), the Lydians issued coins of gold and silver separately.

The ratio in value between gold and silver has been, historically, between 10:1 and 14:1. Transactions with electrum in which the proportions of the two elements varied in each coin would have been difficult if not impossible. Therefore, it did not take long for the Lydians to split the bimetallic electrum into separate gold and silver coinages. After the sack of Sardis, the Lydian capital, by the Persian king Cyrus the Great in 547 B.C., the Persians continued to mint coins, eventually creating a type of the Persian King as a running archer. These coins were known as Darics, after Darius the king, just as the Lydian gold pieces had been known as Croeseids, after King Croesus. The silver coins were called sigloi, equivalent to the Hebrew shekel. It is a curiosity that these Persian coins are found in quantities in western Asia Minor but not in the Persian capital of Persepolis itself. In the foundation deposit at Persepolis, some 1761 miles east of Sardis, impressions of two Darics were made on a clay tablet. The Darics themselves were never found.

PIK

23.
Lydia, time of Alyattes?
ca. 615–561 B.C.

Third-stater (Electrum, 4.71g)

Obv. Forepart of lion, r., with radiate protuberance or "nose-wart" on forehead. To right, faint traces of Lydian inscription: *falfet* (or *walwesh*). This has been taken to mean Alyattes, the father of Croesus.

Rev. Two square incuse punches.

Cornell Classical Collection. No. 669

24.
Achaemenid Kings of Persia
After 450 B.C.

Daric (Gold, 8.34g)

Obv. The Great King kneeling-running right, holding a spear and bow.

Rev. Oblong incuse punch.

Promised gift of Mr. and Mrs. Robert E. Ostrander, Class of 1952

Herbert F. Johnson Museum of Art Collection. 2002.021.002

25.
Achaemenid Kings of Persia
After 450 B.C.

Siglos (Silver, 5.47g)

Obv. The Great King kneeling-running right, holding a spear and bow.

Rev. Oblong incuse punch.

Gift of Mr. Robert E. Ostrander, Class of 1952

Herbert F. Johnson Museum of Art Collection. 98.096.007

All coins reproduced approximately twice actual size except as noted.

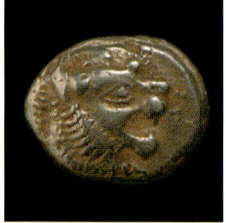

23. Obv.

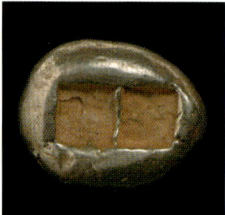

23. Rev.

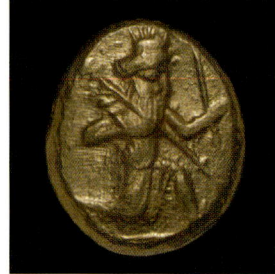

24. Obv.

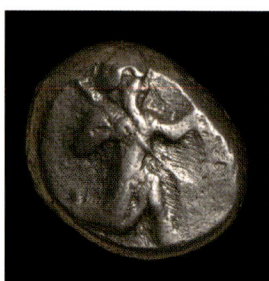

25. Obv

The Lydian invention of coinage was taken up with alacrity by many of the Greek city-states, which preferred silver and hardly ever used gold until the time of Philip II of Macedon in the fourth century B.C. Value depended on weight, and often a common weight standard is the clue to whether two cities were trading with one another or not. Coins of similar type in the Cornell collections often weigh within several hundredths of a gram of one another. The coins of some states became the currency of choice for business transactions around the Greek world and consequently did not change much over a long period of time. Indeed, an Aeginetan "turtle" with a row of dots down its back, like no. 26, was found in the foundation deposit at Persepolis, mentioned earlier. The coins of Aegina, Corinth, and Athens are excellent examples of the retention of conservative and economical designs over centuries.

The Pegasoi of Corinth (no. 28), popular for two and a half centuries, from about 550–300 B.C., albeit with differing and developing modes of representation, were retained by her daughter and granddaughter colonies. The only difference was the substitution of, say, the letter A (for Ambracia, no. 29) or L (for Leukas, no. 30) in place of the Corinthian *qoppa* (our letter Q). The weight standards remained those of the mother city. An oddity of the Corinthian coinage is that Athena is always on the reverse of the coin rather than the obverse.

The Old Style Tetradrachms of Athens (no. 31) are difficult to date precisely. These Athenian "owls" are thought to have begun in about 480 B.C. (the precise date is debated hotly), but their development seems to parallel styles of representation in sculpture and vase painting (cf. the treatment of the eyes or the drapery on the black-figure and red-figure vases, nos. 3, 5-7). Coinage tends to be conservative in style, however, and the coin-using public was probably just as averse to innovation 2,500 years ago as it is now. The New Style Tetradrachms of Athens (no. 32) are particularly informative. This is because, in the Athenian system of reckoning the date, each year was identified by the name of a magistrate, whose only function was to give his name to the year, whence the title "Eponymous" [name-giving].

PIK

26.
Aegina
Sixth century or early fifth century B.C.

Stater (Silver, 11.98g)

Obv. Sea-turtle with smooth shell. (It should have a row of dots down the spine, but these have been obliterated on this coin.) The countermarks punched on the turtle's back suggest that this coin must have traveled sufficiently far from Aegina that a suspicious merchant saw fit to weigh it and revalidate it before accepting it as currency.

Rev. Incuse square with crude 'mill-sail' pattern.

Cornell Classical Collection. No. 38

27.
Aegina
Probably early fourth century B.C.

Stater (Silver, 5.59g)

Obv. Tortoise with shell articulated into 13 squares.

Rev. Incuse square of 'large skew' pattern, divided by straight lines, the principal two of which are perpendicular, into five compartments, the upper right of which contains two pellets.

Cornell Classical Collection. No. 29

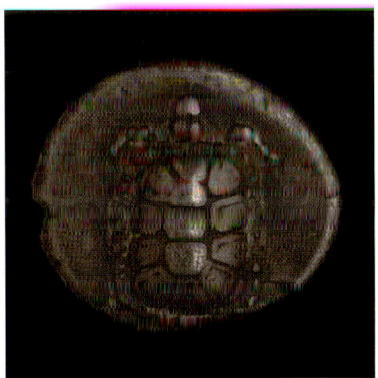

26. Obv.

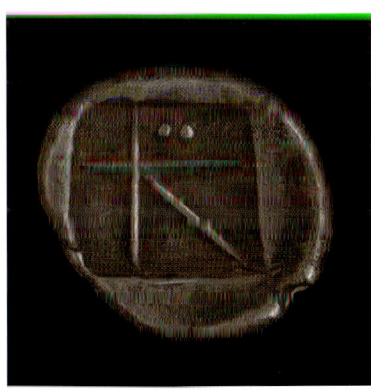

27. Obv.   *27. Rev*

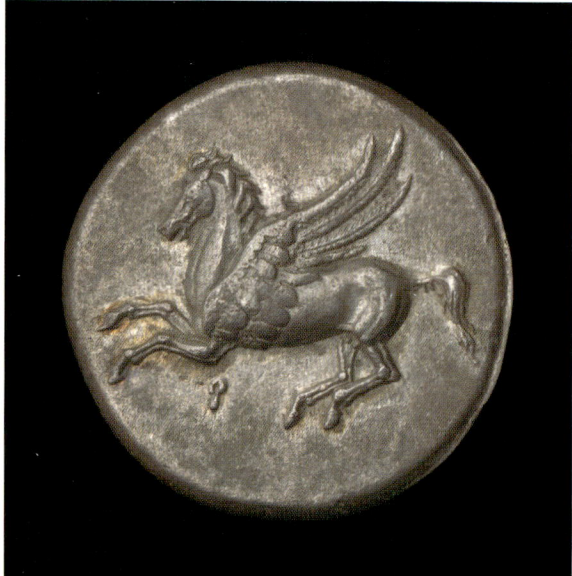

28. Obv.

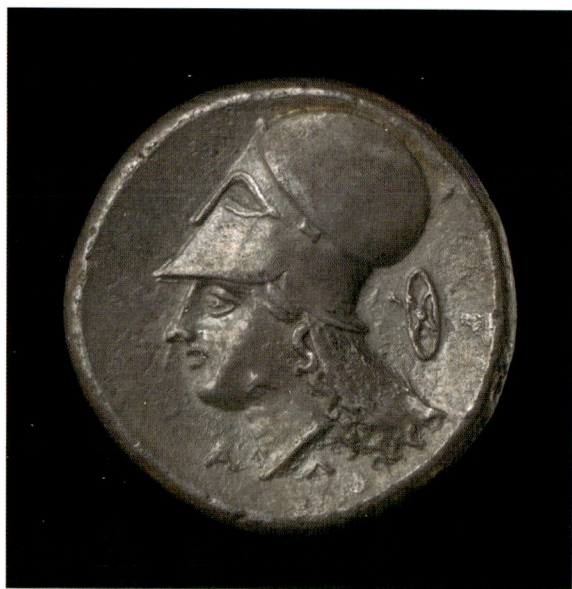

28. Rev

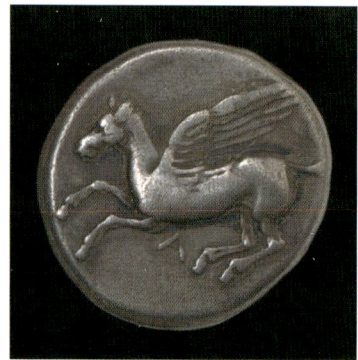

29. Obv.

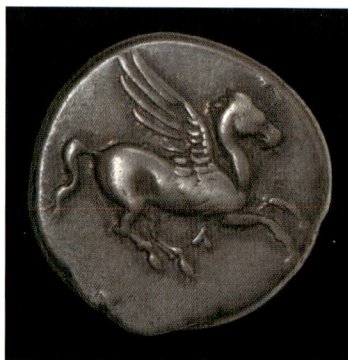

30. Obv.

28.
Corinth
Probably late fourth century B.C.

Stater (Silver, 8.43g)

Obv. Pegasus flying left, *qoppa* (for Corinth) beneath.

Rev. Head of Athena left, wearing Corinthian helmet; wheel with four spokes seen at an angle, right; A beneath Athena's chin.

Gift of Mr. and Mrs. Robert E. Ostrander, Class of 1952.

Herbert F. Johnson Museum of Art Collection. 99.075.008
This coin is reproduced approximately three times its actual size.

29.
Ambracia, Epiros
(Corinthian colony)
ca. 360–338 B.C.

Stater (Silver, 8.20g)

Obv. Pegasus flying left, A beneath.

Rev. Head of Athena left, wearing Corinthian helmet over leather cap; spearhead with mid-rib and E right; A on lappet of Athena's helmet. A in field left.

Cornell Classical Collection. No. 26

30.
Leukas, Akarnania
(Corinthian colony)
ca. 350–300 B.C.

Stater (Silver, 8.45g)

Obv. Pegasus flying right, Λ (for Leukas) beneath.

Rev. Head of Athena right, wearing Corinthian helmet over a leather cap; an amphora, bunch of grapes hanging from vine, and A in field left.

Cornell Classical Collection. No. 179

31.
Athens
Late fifth century B.C.

Old Style Tetradrachm
(Silver, 16.82g)

Obv. Head of Athena right, with a frontal eye but developing some profile characteristics, wearing a crested helmet ornamented with three olive leaves and a floral scroll; her hair drawn across her forehead in parallel curves.

Rev. Owl standing right, head facing, olive spray and crescent to left. ΑΘΕ in large even letters to right, all in incuse square.

Cornell Classical Collection. No. 14

32.
Athens
164/3 B.C.

New Style Tetradrachm
(Silver, 16.95g)

Obv. Helmeted head of Athena right.

Rev: Owl facing, standing on amphora with B, marking the month of issue. ΑΘΕ above. To right: forepart of lion. Magistrates' names: ΔΟΡΟΘΕ−ΔΙΟΦ−ΔΙΟΚΛΕ. In exergue: ΣΦ

Gift of Mr. and Mrs. Robert E. Ostrander, Class of 1952

Herbert F. Johnson Museum of Art Collection. 99.075.006

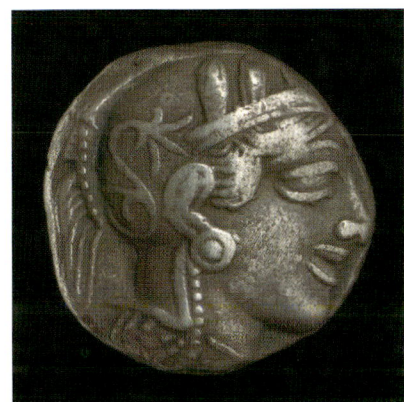

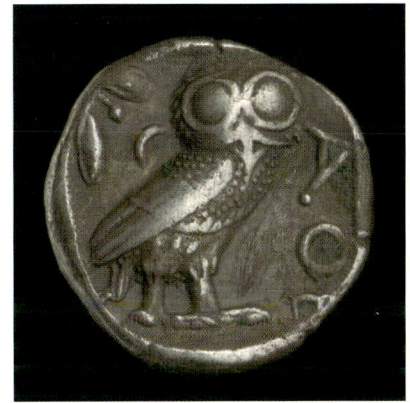

31. Obv.   *31. Rev.*

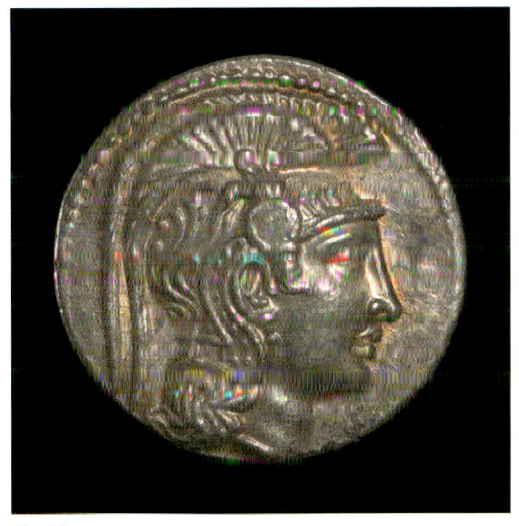

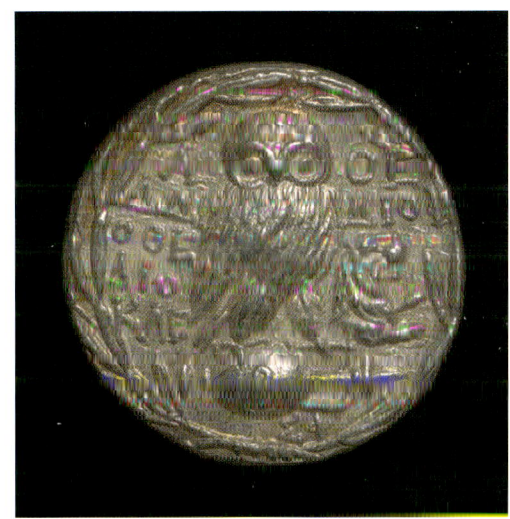

32. Obv.   *32. Rev.*

Symbols or Badges of Cities, Local Mythology

As the turtle was to Aegina, the owl to Athens, and Pegasus to Corinth, so, too, did various deities or symbols become the badges or emblems of other city states. Although the badges had a practical purpose— the guaranteeing of both purity and weight of the metal— it took little time for the die-engravers to create some really imaginative figures. Among them are the coins of the Greek cities in Southern Italy and Sicily, which tended to be highly inventive in design and execution. We select half a dozen from the sixth to the second centuries B.C. that are typical. The Olynthos tetradrachm, with Apollo and the lyre (no. 36), is interesting not only for its iconography and beauty but also because it is a *league* or *alliance* coin, prefiguring the modern Euro coins by some 2,400 years. The labyrinth on the Knossos coin (no. 37), if it is a representation of the Minoan palace, shows that the people of Knossos remembered the story of the Minotaur almost a thousand years after the palace burned to the ground.

PIK

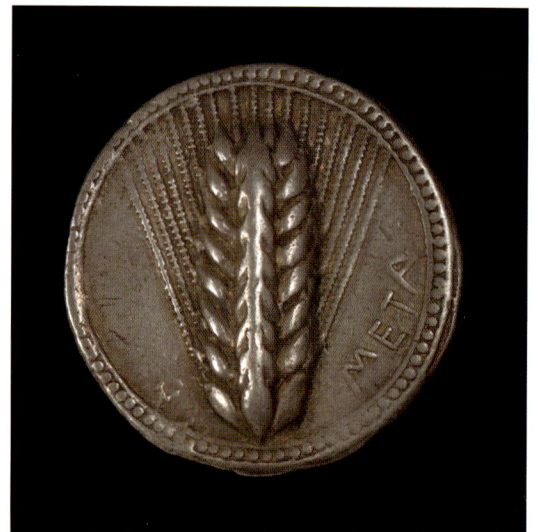

33. Obv.

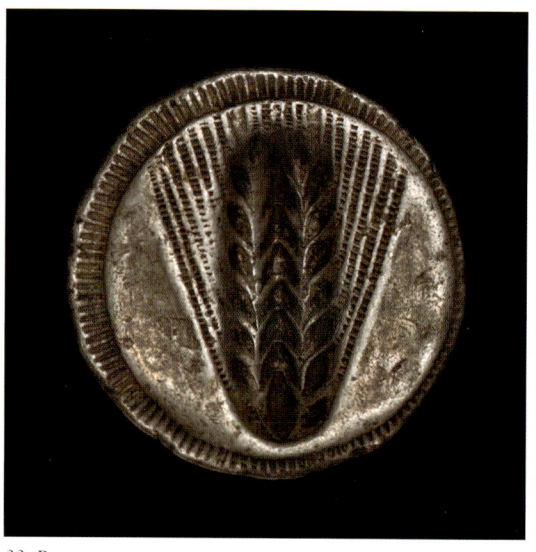

33. Rev.

33.
Metapontum, Lucania
ca. 530–500 B.C.

Stater (Silver, 7.96g) of thin, spread fabric

Obv. Ear of barley in high relief, META to right.

Rev. Same as obverse but incuse and without legend.

Cornell Classical Collection. No. 201

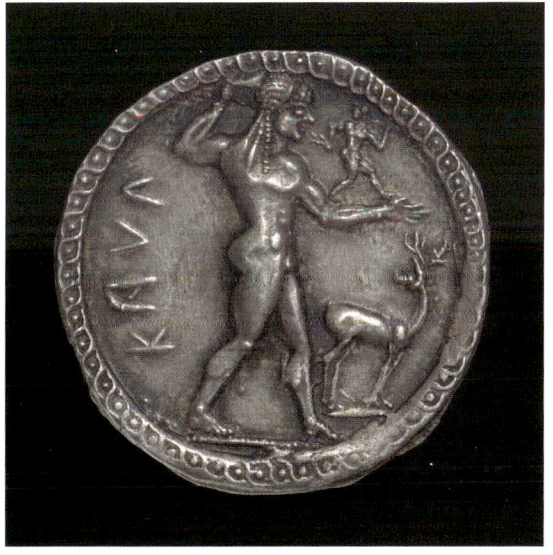

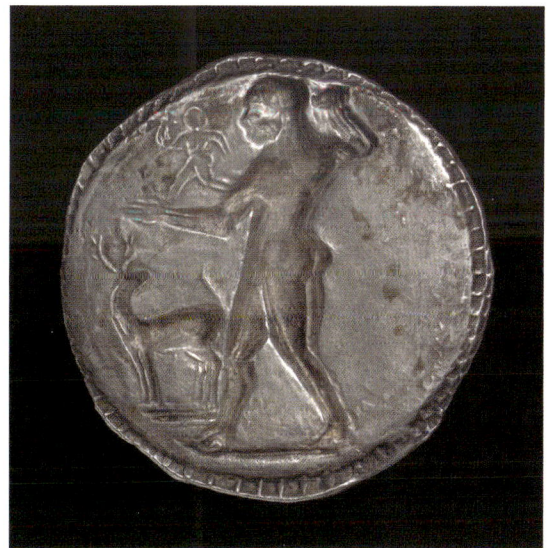

34. Obv.   *34. Rev.*

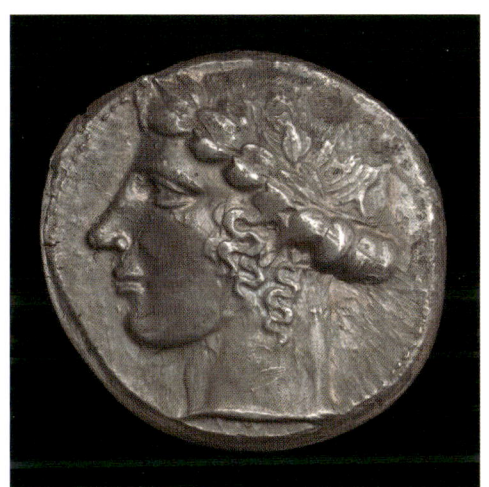

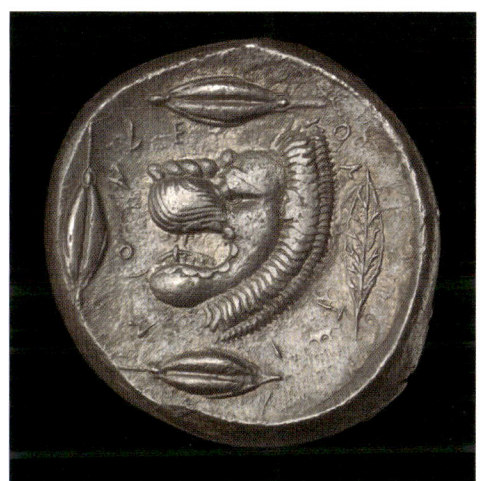

35. Obv.   *35. Rev.*

34.
Kaulonia, Bruttium
ca. 525–480 B.C.

Stater (Silver, 7.77g)

Obv. Apollo, naked, striding right holding a laurel branch in left hand and a small running naked figure, also with a branch, in his outstretched right hand; stag standing on right, looking back; KAVΛ (in left field).

Rev. Same as obverse but incuse and without legend.

Cornell Classical Collection. No. 216

35.
Leontinoi, Sicily
ca. 455–430 B.C.

Tetradrachm (Silver, 17.15g)

Obv. Laureate head of Apollo left.

Rev. Lion head with open jaws; around, three barleycorns and one bay leaf, LEONTINON

Gift of Jerry Theodorou

Herbert F. Johnson Museum of Art Collection. 97.018

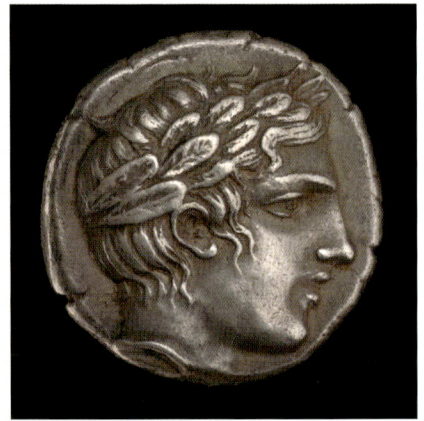

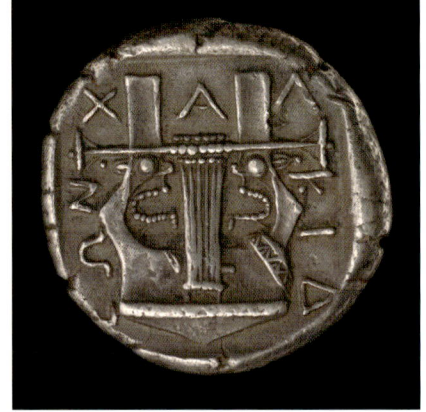

36. Obv.　　　　　　　　　　　　*36. Rev.*

36.
Olynthos, Chalcidian League
ca. 420–355 B.C.

Tetradrachm (Silver, 14.4g)

Obv. Laureate head of Apollo right.

Rev. ΧΑΛΚΙΔΕΩΝ around a
6-string lyre.

Gift of Dr. Robert Caldwell,
Class of 1940

Cornell Classical Collection.
Caldwell-1

37.
Knossos, Crete
ca. 280 B.C.

Stater (Silver, 11.13g)

Obv. Head of Hera left, wearing a
stephanos adorned with palmettes.

Rev. Square Labyrinth, partial A and
arrowhead to left, P above thunderbolt
to right, ΚΝΩΣΙΩΝ below.

Cornell Classical Collection. No. 569

38.
Magnesia on the Maeander, Ionia
ca. 150 B.C.

Tetradrachm (Silver, 16.6g)

Obv. Diademed bust of Artemis right,
bow and quiver at her shoulder.

Rev. Apollo, nude, standing left on a
meander pattern, holding a branch in
his right hand and resting his left
elbow on a tripod surmounted by a
quiver.
ΜΑΓΝΗΤΩΝ ΕΥΦΗΜΟΣ ΠΑΥΣΑΝΙΟΥ. All
within a laurel wreath.

Gift of Mr. and Mrs. Robert E.
Ostrander, Class of 1952.

Herbert F. Johnson Museum of Art
Collection. 2002.021.016

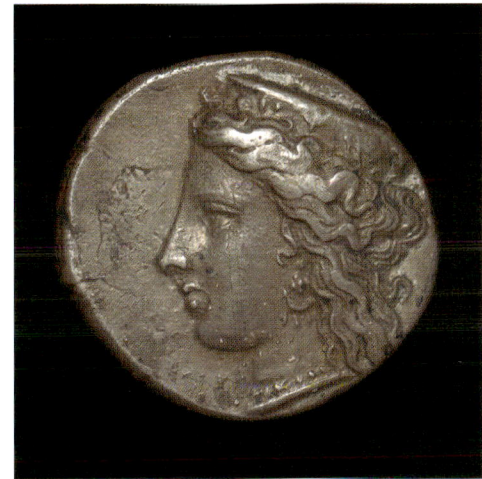

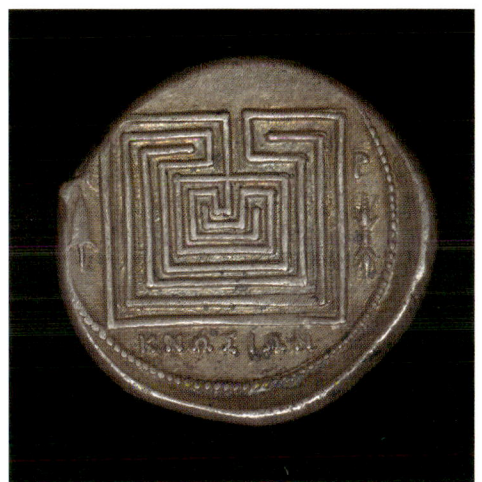

37. Obv.   *37. Rev.*

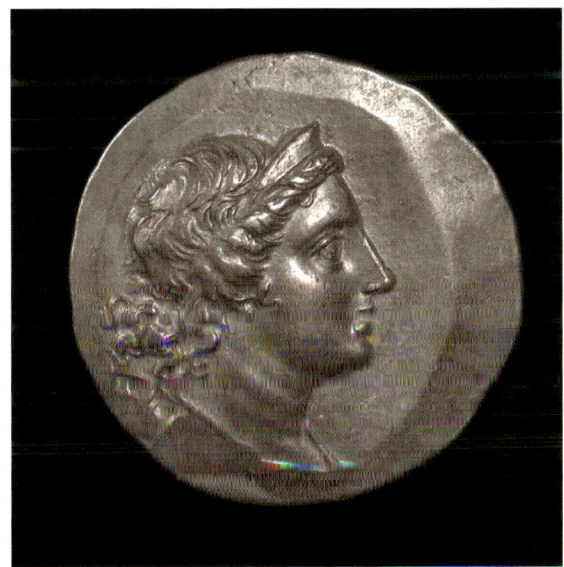

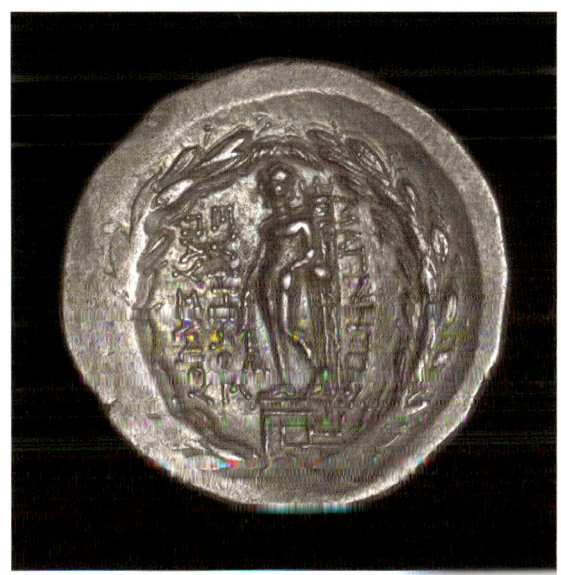

*Alexander, His Immediate
Successors, and Similar Portraits*

The victories of Alexander the Great
over the Persians widened Greek
influence to the east beyond the
Mediterranean, and after his death his
generals carved out new kingdoms
from the remains of his empire. We
show four coins, part of a long-lived
succession extending down to Roman
times. Indeed, the Ptolemy coin (no.
40), on which a generalized representation of Herakles is depicted on the
obverse, might easily be mistaken for
Alexander himself. Almost three centuries after Alexander's death, the
Roman Quaestor Aesillas (no. 42)
legitimized his coin by making sure
the Alexander representation, long
familiar to the citizens of
Thessalonika, was on the obverse.

PIK

39.
Alexander III, the Great
lifetime or early posthumous,
334–300 B.C.

Tetradrachm (Silver, 17.07g)

Obv. Head of Herakles right,
clad in lion's skin.

Rev. Zeus enthroned left with his right
leg drawn back; feet on a stool; holding an eagle in his right hand and a
scepter in his left. Monogram below
eagle, ΚΛ under throne. ΑΛΕΧΑΝΔΡΟΥ
to right. In exergue: ΒΑΣΙΛΕΩΣ

Gift of Mr. and Mrs. Robert E.
Ostrander, Class of 1952.

Herbert F. Johnson Museum of Art
Collection. 2000.024.003

40.
Ptolemy I
323-285 B.C.

Tetradrachm (Silver, 15.73g)

Obv. Head of Herakles right, in
elephant-skin helmet and the horn
of Ammon.

Rev. Athena striding right in crested
helmet, with a spear and shield raised,
stacked drapery folds; ΔΙ, eagle, and a
Corinthian helmet in field right.
ΑΛΕΧΑΝΔΡΟΥ to left.

Cornell Classical Collection. No. 832

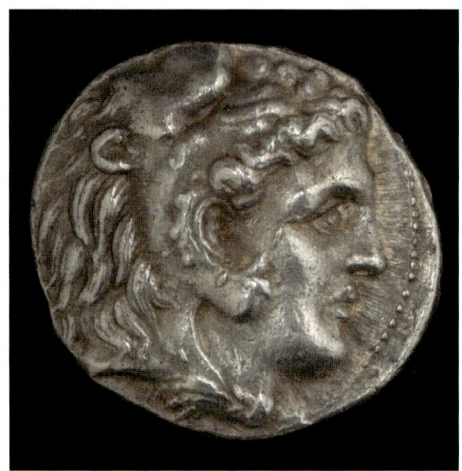
39. Obv.

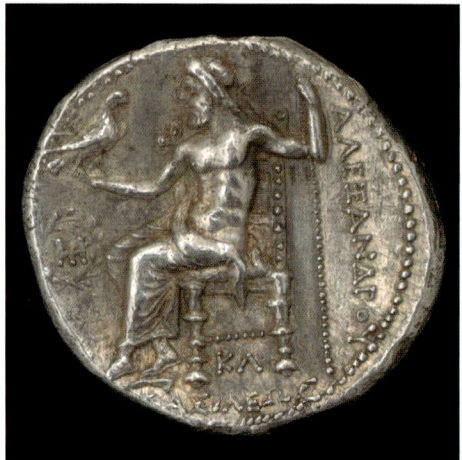
39. Rev.

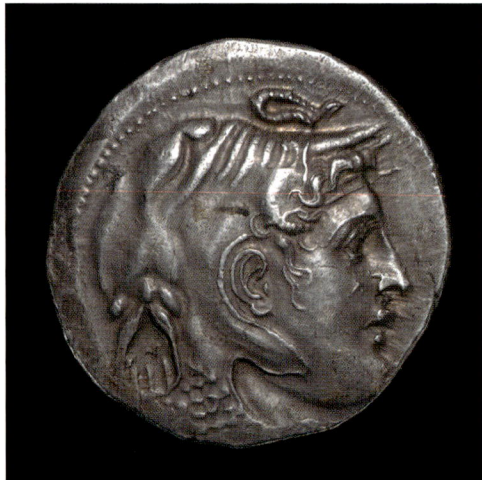
40. Obv.

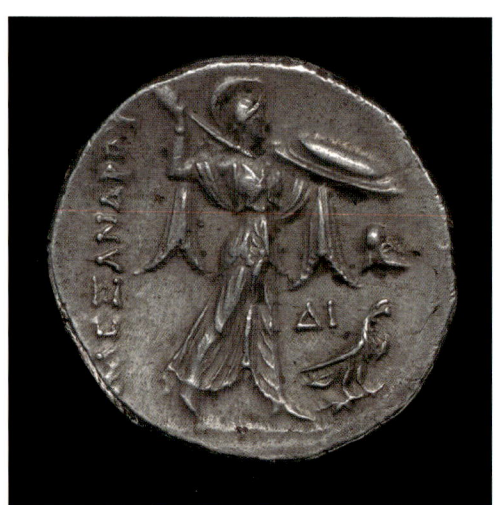
40. Rev.

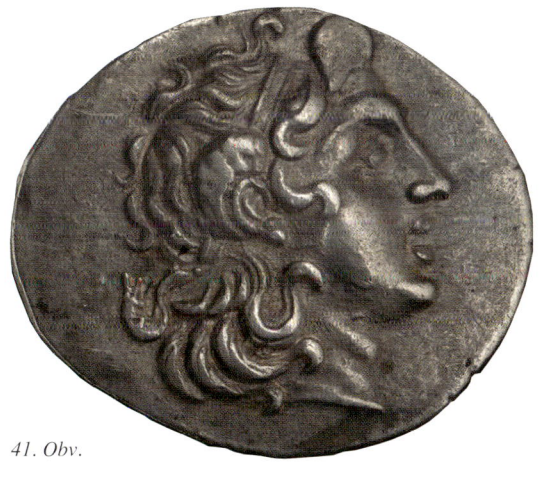

41. Obv.

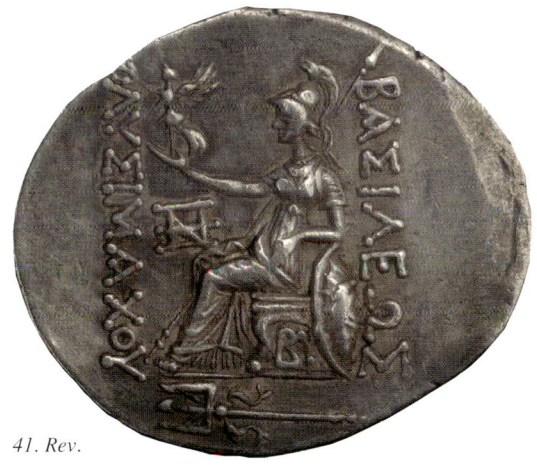

41. Rev.

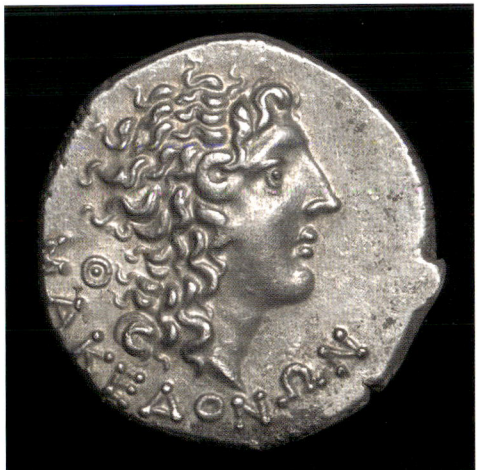

42. Obv.

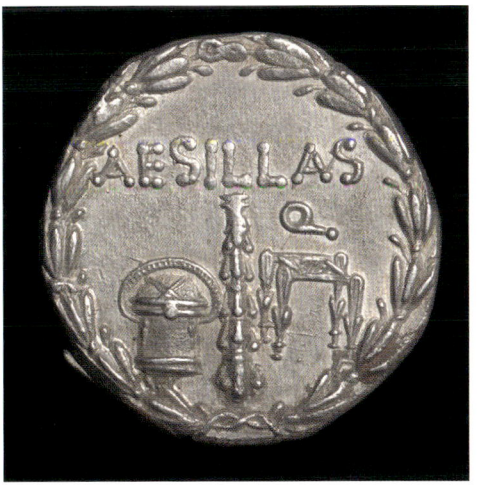

42. Rev.

41.
Lysimachos
ca. 297–281 B.C.

Large Flan Tetradrachm (Silver, 16.86g)

Obv. Diademed head of Alexander
right, wearing horns of Ammon. This
is normally considered the most reli-
able portrait of Alexander.

Rev. Athena seated left resting left
arm on shield and with Nike in out
stretched right hand. BY under throne
for Byzantium, where the coin was
minted. transverse spear resting against
her right side. ΒΑΣΙΛΕΩΣ ΛΥΣΙΜΑΧΟΥ
Monogram in field left. In exergue, a
trident

Promised gift of Mr. and Mrs. Robert
E. Ostrander, Class of 1952

Herbert F. Johnson Museum of Art
Collection, 2002.021.024

42. Macedonia under the Romans
ca. 93–88 B.C.

Tetradrachm (Silver, 16.26g)

Obv. Head of deified Alexander the
Great, right, with horn of Ammon and
flowing hair, MAKEΔΟΝΩΝ beneath. Θ
behind head (mint of Thessalonika).

Rev. Money chest, club, quaestor's
stool; above all AESILLAS Q (for
Quaestor, the financial assistant to the
Roman Governor); all within a laurel
wreath.

Cornell Classical Collection, No. 1460

Ptolemaic Kingdom of Egypt, Gold Issues

Splendid additions to this series of royal portraits are some unusual gold coins in large denominations issued by the Macedonian kings of Egypt who created the dynasty of the Ptolemies. The size of the flans on which the portraits were struck allows for some fine detail.

PIK

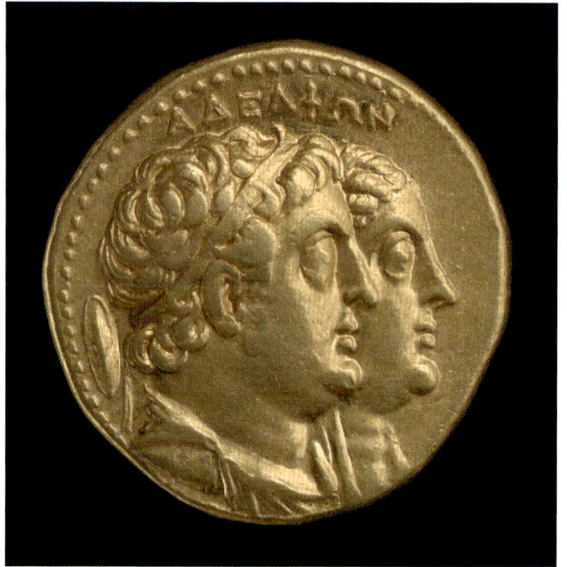

43. Obv.

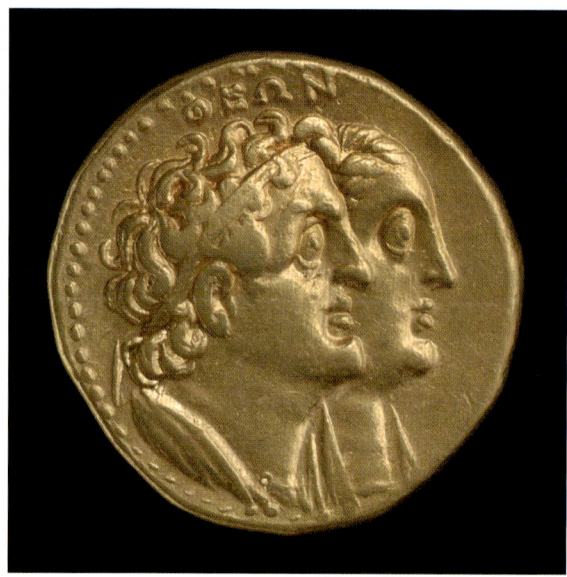

43. Rev.

43.
Ptolemy II, Philadelphos
285–246 B.C.

Commemorative Octadrachm
(Gold, 27.69g)

Obv. Conjoined busts right of Ptolemy II, diademed and draped, and Arsinoe II, diademed and veiled; above, ΑΔΕΛΦΩΝ meaning "[image of the] brother and sister"; behind, shield.

Rev. Conjoined busts right of Ptolemy I, diademed, and Berenike I, diademed and veiled; above ΘΕΩΝ.

Gift of Mr. Joseph Silbert, Class of 1915.

Cornell Classical Collection.
Silbert-27
This coin is reproduced at approximately 230% of its actual size.

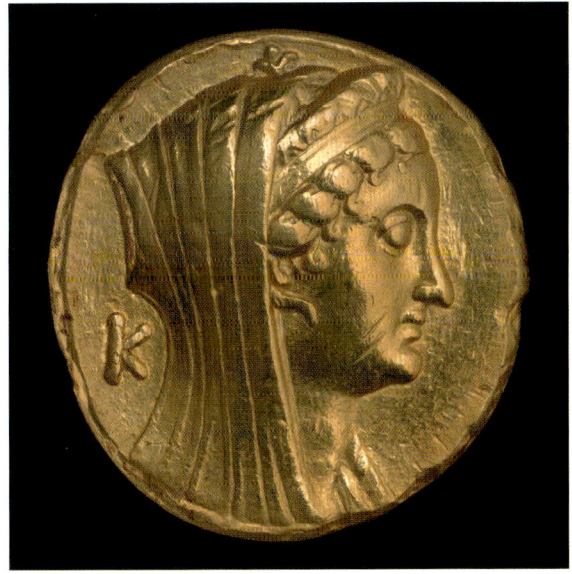

44. Obv.

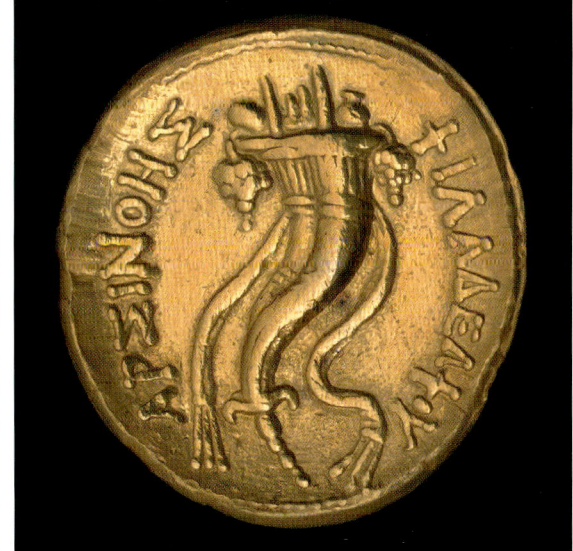

44. Rev.

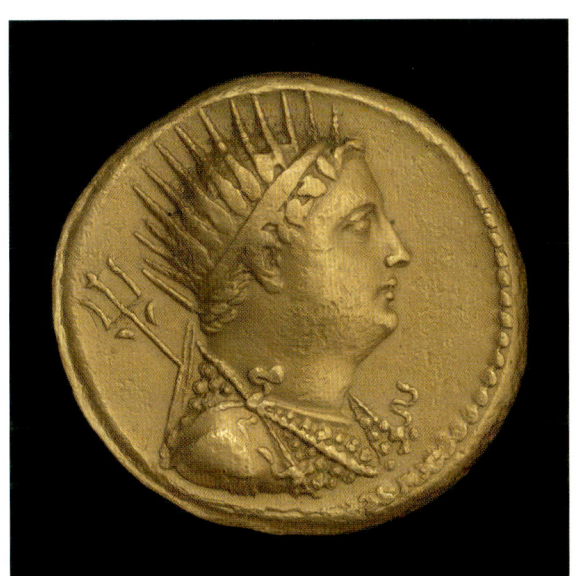

45. Obv.

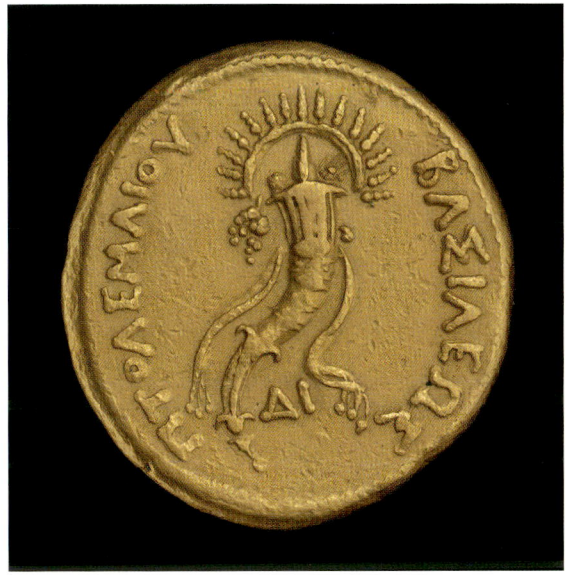

45. Rev.

44.
Arsinoe II, sister-wife of Ptolemy II, Philadelphos
ca. 285–246 B.C.

Octadrachm (Gold, 27.81g)

Obv. Veiled head of Arsinoe II right, wearing stephane (crown), scepter behind head visible above, K in left field. (Probably annual sequence mark)

Rev. ΑΡΣΙΝΟΗΣ ΦΙΛΑΔΕΛΦΟΥ, Double cornucopiae bound with fillet.

Gift of Mr. and Mrs. Robert F. Ostander, Class of 1952.

Herbert F. Johnson Museum of Art Collection, 2000.024.012

This coin is reproduced at approximately 230% of its actual size.

45.
Ptolemy IV, Philopator
221–205 B.C.

Octadrachm (Gold, 27.75g)

Obv. Radiate bust of Ptolemy III right, wearing an aegis, trident over left shoulder.

Rev. Radiate cornucopia, bound with fillet, ΔΙ below.
ΒΑΣΙΛΕΩΣ ΠΤΟΛΕΜΑΙΟΥ

Cornell Classical Collection, No. 836

This coin is reproduced at approximately 230% of its actual size.

The idea of including portraiture of living monarchs on the coins took root in the expanding Greek world of the fourth century B.C., especially where there was already some local tradition of depicting a ruler. Philip and Alexander had provided the basis for a brilliant beginning to a long series of royal portraits captured in superb detail on sizeable silver coins whose range extended over three centuries and as far as Western India. As time and distance from fourth century Macedon expands, the "Greekness" of the portraiture, not to mention the inscriptions, sometimes becomes a bit difficult to recognize at a glance.

PIK

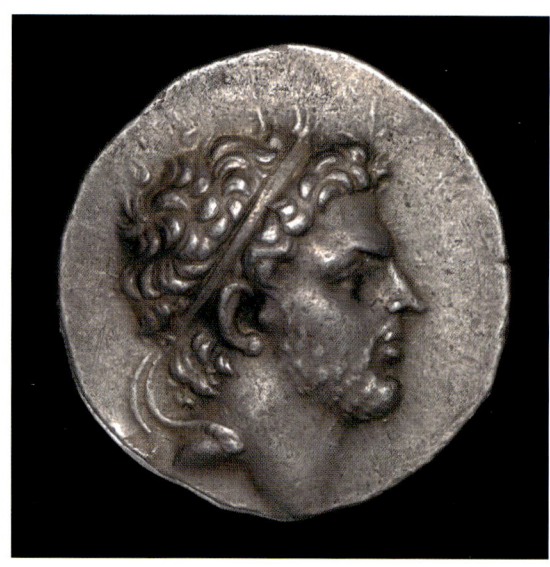

46. Obv.

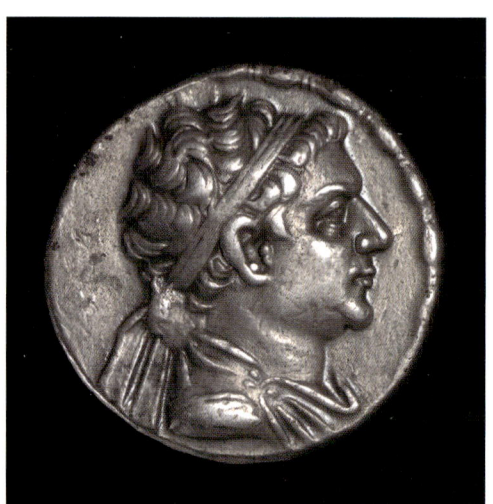

47. Obv.

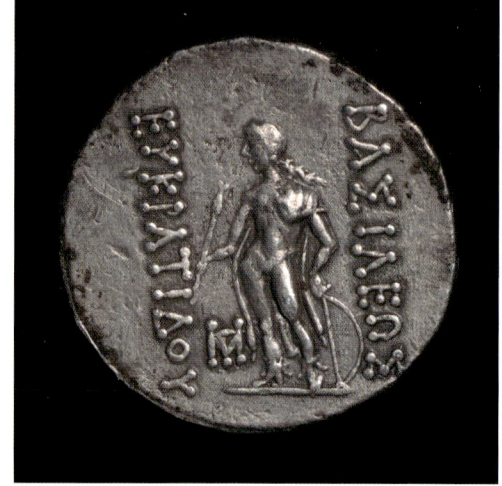

47. Rev.

46.
Perseus, King of Macedon
179–168 B.C.

Tetradrachm (Silver, 15.18g)

Obv. Diademed head of Perseus right with close beard.

Rev. Eagle, wings open, standing right on a thunderbolt. ΒΑΣΙΛΕΩΣ ΠΕΡΣΕΩΣ across field and three monograms: above head Ξ, between feet Λ, in field right ΑΤ. All within an oak wreath; a plough beneath.

Cornell Classical Collection. No. 316

47.
Eukratides, King of Bactria
171–135 B.C.

Stater (Silver, 16.92g)

Obv. Diademed and draped bust of Eukratides right, in a bead and reel border.

Rev. Figure with a fillet standing left on ground line, holding an arrow/spear in right hand, bow in left. ΒΑΣΙΛΕΩΣ ΕΥΚΡΑΤΙΔΟΥ

Cornell Classical Collection. 2-S

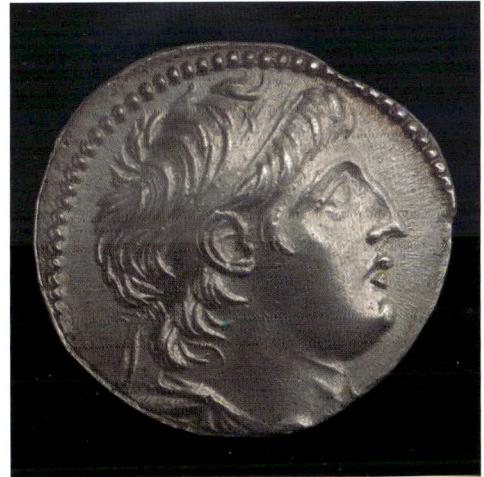

48. Obv.

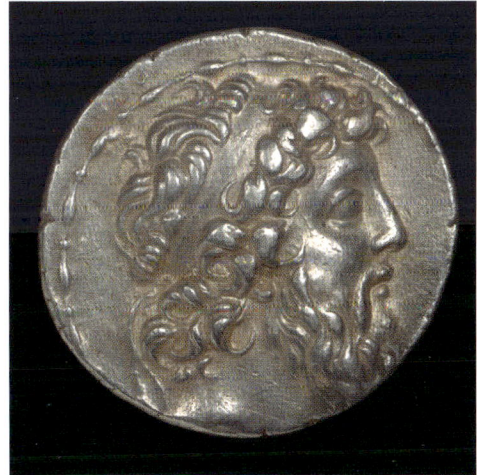

49. Obv.

48.
Antiochos VII, Euergetes (Sidetes),
King of Syria
ca. 138–129 B.C.

Tetradrachm (Silver, 13.8g)
(Phoenician standard)

Obv. Diademed and draped bust of
Antiochos VII right, in a border of
dots.

Rev. Eagle standing left on the beak of
a galley, palm branch in the background. ΒΑΣΙΛΕΩΣ ΑΝΤΙΟΧΟΥ and
monograms.

Gift of Mr. and Mrs. Robert E.
Ostrander, Class of 1952.

Herbert F. Johnson Museum of Art
Collection. 2002.021.015

49.
Demetrios II, Nikator, King of Syria
129-125 B.C., second reign

Tetradrachm (Silver, 16.75g)

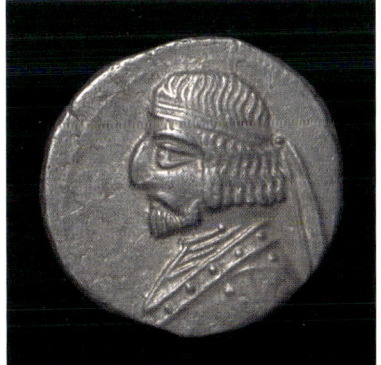

50. Obv.

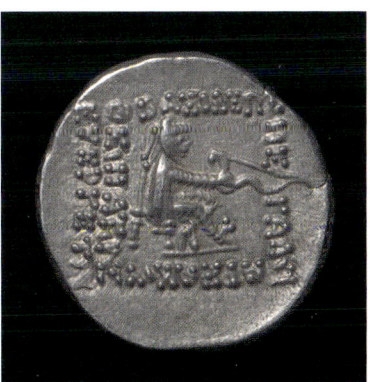

50. Rev.

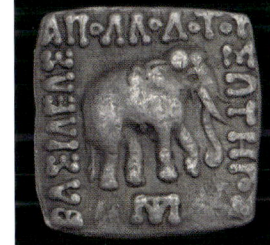

51. Obv.

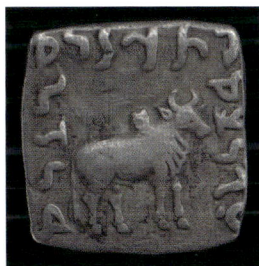

51. Rev.

Obv. Diademed and bearded head of
Demetrios II to right, in a bead and
reel border.

Rev. Zeus enthroned, facing left, holding Nike in his left hand and a scepter
in his right. ΒΑΣΙΛΕΩΣ ΔΗΜΗΤΡΙΟΥ
ΘΕΟΥ ΝΙΚΑΤΟΡΟΣ ΙΙ

Gift of Mr. and Mrs. Robert E.
Ostrander, Class of 1952.

Herbert F. Johnson Museum of Art
Collection. 2002.021.001

50.
Gotarzes I, King of Parthia
ca. 80–70 B.C.

Drachm (Silver, 4.17g)

Obv. Bust of Gotarzes left with a
diademed head, long hair and short
beard

Rev. Archer (originally Apollo) seated
right on an omphalos, holding a bow.
ΒΑΣΙΛΕΟΣ ΜΕΓΑΛΟΥ ΑΡΣΑΚΟΥ
ΘΕΟΠΑΤΟΡΟΣ ΕΥΕΡΓΕΤΟΥ

Cornell Classical Collection. 1 8

51.
Apollodotos I, Indo-Greek King
ca. 160–150 B.C.

Drachm, square,
Indo-Greek standard (Silver, 2.36g)

Obv. Elephant walking right
ΒΑΣΙΛΕΩΣ ΑΠΟΛΛΟΔΟΤΟΥ ΣΩΤΗΡΟΣ

Rev. Humped bull; Kharosthi legend
more or less equivalent to the Greek
on the obverse except that Apollodotos
is now called a Maharajah

Cornell Classical Collection. No. 827

In contrast to that of the Greeks, the Roman and other Italic economies were based on the use of copper, and they were slow to mint in silver until economic and strategic relations required it. The first copper pieces were shapeless lumps, apparently broken off the raw lump (known as the 'pig,' as in pig iron) from the smelter. These were later transformed into coins, where the unit, an as, was originally one pound (libra=lb.) of copper; the early coins were cast rather than struck.

Roman coinage is often disparaged when it is compared to that of the Greeks, but in fact the Romans struck a remarkable series of emperors' portraits in gold, silver, and brass for a coinage that was standardized over a very wide area. After the civil wars, in which both sides had sporadically issued coins, the emperor Augustus (no. 12) reorganized the coinage. In particular, he regularized the issue of gold pieces so that there were forty-two to a pound of gold, and he introduced two large coin denominations in brass, the sestertius (four asses) and the dupondius (two asses). These were technically issued by the Senate, whence the SC (*ex senatus consulto* or "by decree of the Senate"), normally found on the reverses (nos. 55-58). These denominations lasted until the third century, when they were given up in the face of galloping inflation, and the whole monetary system was repeatedly reorganized.

A silver denarius of the Emperor Tiberius (no. 52), with his head on the obverse and the figure of Pax (the personification of peace) seated on the reverse, is a fine example of far-flung distribution. The portrait was immediately recognizable as that of the Roman emperor, as we learn from the Gospel of St. Matthew 22:20-21, where Jesus used the portrait on a denarius to confound the Pharisees. They were trying to trick him by asking if it was right to pay the census tribute to the emperor, who is called, generically, "Caesar:"

> 20: And he saith unto them, Whose is this image and superscription?
> 21: They say unto him, Caesar's. Then saith he unto them, Render therefore unto Caesar the things which are Caesar's; and unto God the things that are God's.

A different view of Pax can be seen in these reverses from coins of Elagabalus and Maximinus (nos. 53, 54): the first with Pax rushing to the left holding a remarkably stylized laurel branch; the second showing Pax standing with a more conventional laurel branch. A more elegant portrait of Maximinus is pictured below (no. 58) on a squarish sestertius with a thick patina.

Both of these examples are part of the Salton Collection, a recent gift to the Museum, which offers the possibility of studying the variety of representations of personifications like Pax, either offered as abstract entities in their own right, or pertaining to a particular emperor.

AR

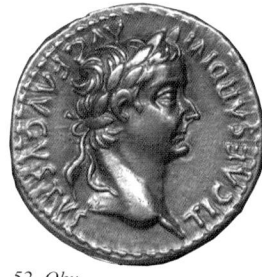 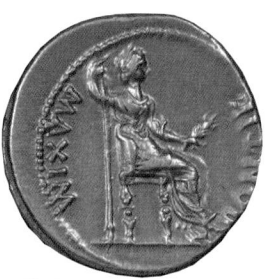

52. Obv.   *52. Rev.*

52.
Tiberius (A.D. 14-37)
ca. A.D. 20

Denarius "Tribute Penny"
(Silver, 3.8g)

Obv. Laureate head of Tiberius, right; TI CAESAR DIVI   AVG F AVGVSTVS counterclockwise.

Rev. Pax seated to right on an elaborate chair holding a laurel branch in her left hand and resting her right hand on a staff; PONTIF MAXIM counterclockwise. All within a border of dots.

Cornell Classical Collection. No. 1210

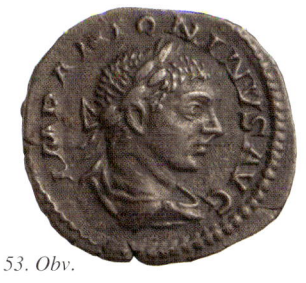

53. Obv.

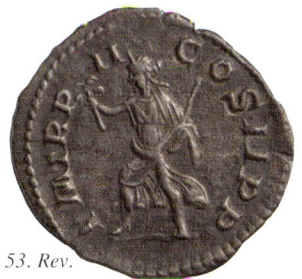

53. Rev.

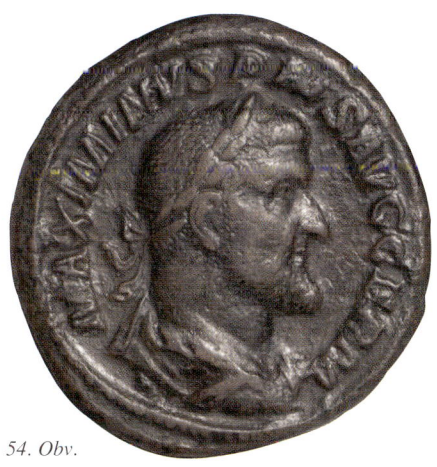

54. Obv.

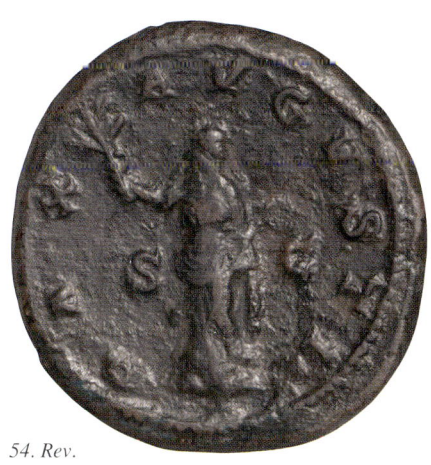

54. Rev.

53.
Elagabalus (A.D. 218–222)
A.D. 219

Denarius (Silver, 2.98g)

Obv: Draped and laureate Elagabalus right. IMP ANTONINVS AVG.

Rev: Pax lunging left with a scepter in her left hand and an olive branch in her right. PM TR P II COS II PP,

Gift of Mark M. and Lottie Dalton

Herbert F. Johnson Museum of Art Collection 2000.175.140

54.
Maximinus I, Thrax (A.D. 235–238)
A.D. 235–238

As (10.42g)

Obv. Draped and laureate Maximinus right. MAXIMINVS PIVS AVG GERM,

Rev. Pax standing with a scepter in her left hand and an olive branch in her right. PAX AVGVSTI.

Gift of Mark M. and Lottie Dalton

Herbert F. Johnson Museum of Art. 2000.175.144

The formula of the Emperor's head (or that of a family member) on the obverse and an allegorical design on the reverse is quite standard on imperial coins. Yet these coins do not exclude specific reference to military campaigns, victory, or buildings, as we can see from some of our pieces. For example, on the fine sestertius of Nero, pictured below (no. 55), the obverse type is a portrait, but the reverse shows a scene of Nero with a spear on a rearing horse accompanied by a horseman with a fluttering standard. Under the ground line the scene is labeled, 'Decursio.' This is actually the Latin term for a military training exercise: the Romans' equivalent of war games practiced either by the infantry, the cavalry, or both. The long inscription around his head includes his names, his successes, and his official and honorific titles. These abbreviations of a language that was already economical can be expanded to be read as: Nero Claudius Caesar Augustus (names and title), Germanicus (success over the Germans) Pontifex Maximus (Chief Priest) Tribunicia Potestate (with the power of a Tribune of the People) Imperator (General) Pater Patriae (Father of the Fatherland).

A very strong profile portrait of Trajan with finely nuanced relief marks the obverse of no. 56. It corresponds closely with several of his portraits in other media. The inscription (COS IIII) on the reverse pins down the date precisely to the year in which he was acclaimed consul for the fourth time.

Caracalla almost always has a grim frowning look in his portraits, appropriate to his character as presented by ancient historians and biographers as seen on no. 57. The female figure on the reverse represents 'Providentia' his hopes for the future.

The obverse of no. 58 is an expressive portrait of Maximinus showing the close-cropped hair and beard that became standard for third century portraits. It may owe something to later likenesses of Caracalla, as in the previous figure. The reverse refers to the military success for which he gained the title Germanicus that is inscribed on the obverse.

AR

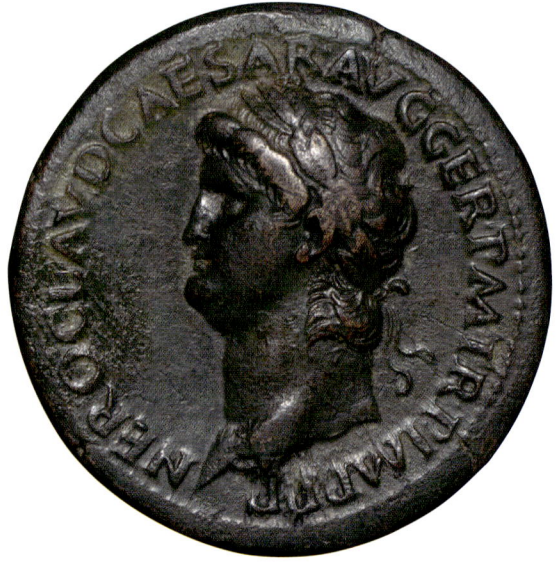

55. Obv.

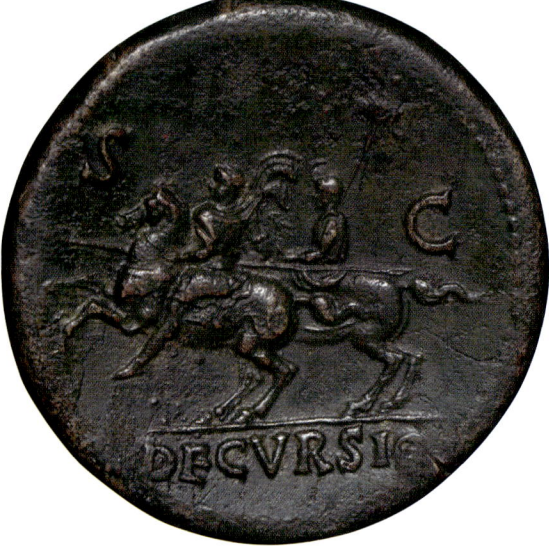

55. Rev.

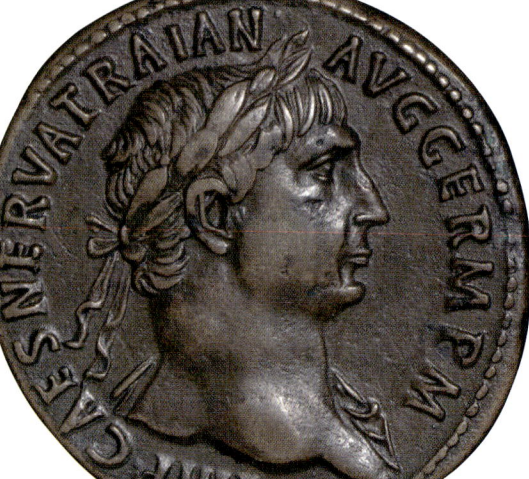

56. Obv.

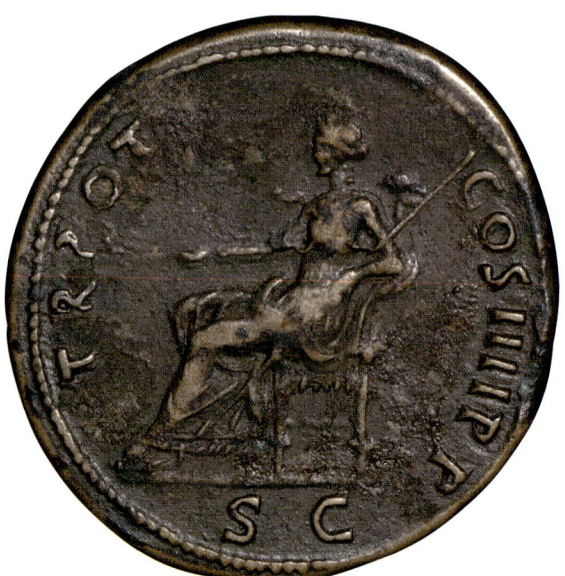

56. Rev.

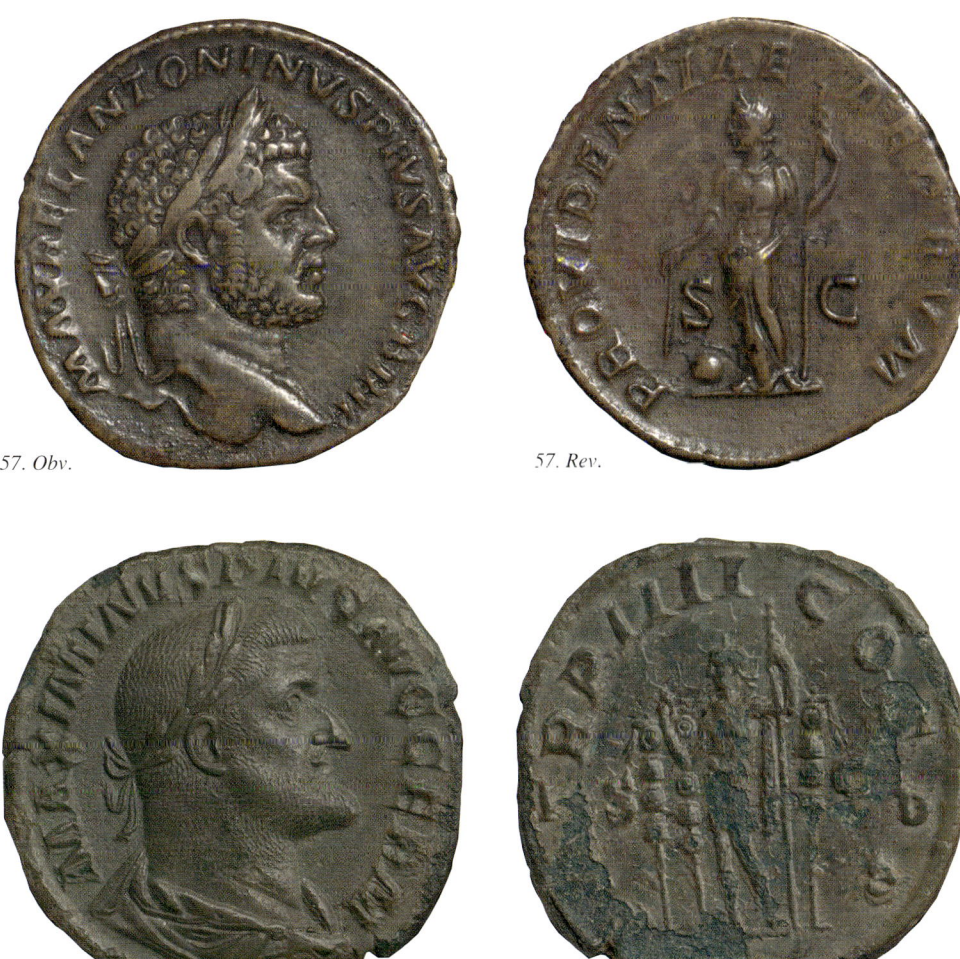

57. Obv.   *57. Rev.*

58. Obv.   *58. Rev.*

55.
Nero (A.D. 54-68)
A.D. 64-68

Sestertius (Brass, 27.96g)

Obv. Laureate bust of Nero left. NERO
CLAVD CAESAR AVG GER PM TR P IMP PP

Rev. Nero and accompanying soldier
galloping left with a spear and standard. S C above; DECVRSIO below.

Cornell Classical Collection. No. 1169

56.
Trajan (A.D. 98–117)
A.D. 101

Sestertius (Brass, 24.38g)

Obv. Laureate and draped bust of
Trajan right. IMP CAES NERVA TRAIAN
AVG GERM PM

Rev: Female figure seated left with
her right hand outstretched, a spear
couched in crook of her left elbow;
TR POT COS IIII PP; below S C.

Cornell Classical Collection. No. 1203

57.
Caracalla (A.D. 198 217)
A.D. 212-217

Sestertius (Brass, 19.94g)

Rome

Obv. Laureate bust of Caracalla right.
M AVREL ANTONINVS PIVS AVG BRIT

Rev: Caracalla standing left, holding a
spear in his left hand and a baton in
his right; a globe at his feet.
PROVIDENTIAE DEORVM S C

Cornell Classical Collection. No. 1340

58.
Maximinus I, Thrax (A.D. 235–238)
A.D. 238

Sestertius (Brass, 16.54g)

Obv: Laureate, draped, and cuirassed
bust of Maximinus right. MAXIMINUS
PIVS AVG GERM

Rev: Maximinus standing left holding
a spear; two standards to the left, one
to the right, flanked by S C;
[PM] TR P IIII COS PP

Cornell Classical Collection. No. 1172

This coin of Maximian (no. 59), usually known to us as Galerius, to avoid confusion with Maximian I, Diocletian's first colleague in his reorganized government, shows the close-shaven head of the emperor crowned with a laurel wreath on the obverse. On the reverse, a female figure identified as Moneta (the Mint) stands, holding balanced scales and a *cornucopia*, or horn of plenty. The follis was a new denomination, containing about four percent silver, and was introduced by Galerius's colleague and superior, Diocletian. This coin has been dated to about A.D. 302 and illustrates the formal "cubist" style for the emperor, while maintaining the traditional classical format for the figure of Moneta.

*

Roman coinage continued after more reorganization under Constantine the Great, one of Galerius's colleagues and successors, who later moved the capital of the Roman Empire to Byzantium. This ancient city was renamed Constantinopolis and eventually became the capital of what we know as the Byzantine Empire, even though the inhabitants insisted they were still Rhomaioi, or Romans. There were two distinct changes of style, first under Constantine and his successors when most of the coins (especially the copper) become small-er and flatter. At this time many of the reverse types have a cross in the center, referring to Christianity as the official religion. Then at the very end of the fifth century A.D., where numismatists place the beginning of Byzantine coinage, there is a dramatic change in the presentations of the imperial portraits. Now they gaze out, full-faced and stiff: icons in miniature.

AR

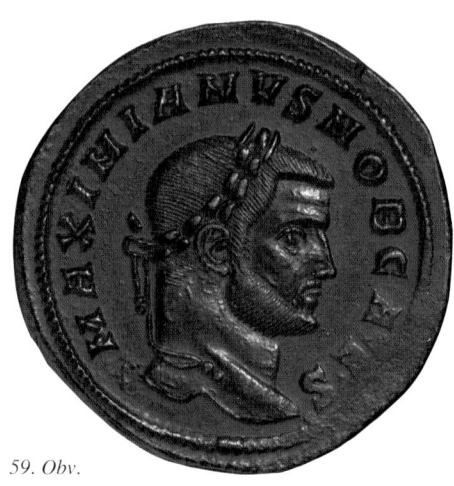

59. Obv.

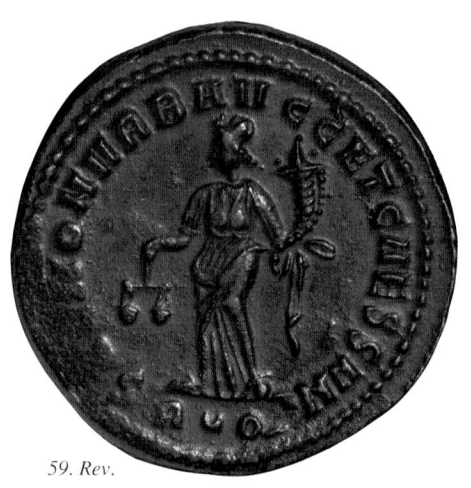

59. Rev.

59.
Maximianus II
(Title of Caesar in A.D. 292)
ca. A.D. 302

Follis (Copper, 12.29g)

Obv. Laureate and cuirassed bust of Maximianus right. MAXIMIANVS NOB CAES

Rev: Moneta standing left holding a balance in right hand and cornucopia in left. SAC MON VRB AVGG ET CAESS NN; below A curly device Q (mint of Aquileia at the head of the Adriatic Sea)

Cornell Classical Collection. No. 1239

SUGGESTIONS FOR FURTHER READING

Barlow, Jane A., and John E. Coleman. "Orestes and Electra at Cornell," *American Journal of Archaeology*,1979.

Beard, Mary, and John Henderson. *Classical Art From Greece to Rome*. Oxford: Oxford University Press, 2001.

Boardman, John. *Early Greek Vase Painting*. London: Thames and Hudson, 1998.

Bonfante, Larissa, ed. *Etruscan Life and Afterlife*. Detroit, MI: Wayne State University Press, 1986.

Colledge, Malcolm A.R. *The Art of Palmyra*. Boulder, CO: Westview Press and London: Thames and Hudson, 1976.

Fairbanks, Arthur. *Athenian White Lekythoi*. Humanistic Series, vol. VI. New York, NY: University of Michigan Studies, 1907.

Fantham, Elaine, and Helene Peet Foley, Natalie Boymel Kampen, Sarah B. Pomeroy, and H. Alan Shapiro. *Women in the Classical World*. Oxford: Oxford University Press, 1994.

Fullerton, Mark D. *Greek Art*. Cambridge: Cambridge University Press, 2000.

de Grummond, Nancy Thomson. *Etruscan Myth, Sacred History, and Legend*. Philadelphia: University of Pennsylvania Museum of Archaeology and Anthropology 2006.

Haynes, Sibyl. *Etruscan Civilization: A Cultural History*. Los Angeles, CA: The J. Paul Getty Museum, 2000.

Herbert F. Johnson Museum of Art, *A Handbook of the Collection*: Ithaca, NY: Herbert F. Johnson Museum of Art, Cornell University, 1998.

Kleiner, Diana E. E. *Roman Sculpture*. New Haven, CT and London: Yale University Press 1992.

Kleiner, Diana E. E., and Susan B. Matheson. *I, Claudia: Women in Ancient Rome*. New Haven, CT: Yale University Art Gallery, 1996.

Kleiner, Fred S. *A History of Roman Art*. Belmont, CA: Thomson/ Wadsworth 2007.

Kraay, Colin M. *Archaic and Classical Greek Coins*. Berkeley, CA: University of California Press, 1976.

Kraay, Colin M. and Max Hirmer. *Greek Coins*. New York, NY: Harry N. Abrams, Inc., 1966.

Kurtz, D. C. *Athenian White Lekythoi*. Oxford: Clarendon Press, 1975.

Ling, Roger. *Ancient Mosaics*. London: British Museum Press, 1998.

Mertens, Joan R. *How to Read Greek Vases*. New York: Metropolitan Museum 2010.

Neils, Jenifer. *The British Museum Concise Introduction to Ancient Greece*. Ann Arbor, MI and London: University of Michigan Press and British Museum Press, 2008.

Newby, Martine and Kenneth Painter. *Roman Glass: Two Centuries of Art and Invention*. London: Society of Antiquaries, 1991.

Pedley, John Griffiths. *Greek Art and Archaeology*. Upper Saddle River, NJ: Prentice Hall, 2007, 4th ed.

Ramage, Andrew. *Emblems of Authority: Greek and Roman Coins from Two Alumni Collections*. Ithaca, NY: Herbert F. Johnson Museum of Art, Cornell University, 1994.

Ramage, Nancy H. and Andrew Ramage. *The British Museum Concise Introduction to Ancient Rome*. Ann Arbor, MI and London: University of Michigan Press and British Museum Press, 2008.

Ramage, Nancy H. and Andrew Ramage. *Roman Art: Romulus to Constantine*. Upper Saddle River, NJ: Prentice Hall, 2009, 5th ed.

Ridgway, Brunilde S. *Roman Copies of Greek Sculpture: The Problem of the Originals*. Ann Arbor, MI: The University of Michigan Press, 1984.

Sparkes, Brian A. *Greek Pottery: An Introduction*. Manchester: Manchester University Press, 1991.

Sparkes, Brian A. *The Red and the Black: Studies in Greek Pottery*. London and New York, NY: Routledge, 1996.

Strong, Donald and David Brown, eds. *Roman Crafts*. New York, NY: New York University Press, 1976.

Szabó, M. *Archaic Terracottas of Boeotia. Rome*, 1994.

Tingay, G.I.F., and J. Badcock. *These Were The Romans*. Chester Springs, PA: Dufour Editions, 1989, 2nd ed.

Toynbee, J.M.C. *Death and Burial in the Roman World*. London: Thames and Hudson, 1971.

Trendall, A.D. *Red Figure Vases of South Italy and Sicily*. London: Thames and Hudson, 1989.

Woodford, Susan. *Images of Myths in Classical Antiquity*. Cambridge: Cambridge University Press, 2002.

Woodford, Susan. *The Trojan War in Ancient Greek Art*. Ithaca, NY: Cornell University Press, 1993.

Zanker, Paul. *The Power of Images in the Age of Augustus*. Ann Arbor, MI: University of Michigan Press, 1988.

This book was designed
by Gilbert Design Associates
Providence, Rhode Island.

The type is Times Roman[T].

The book was printed and bound
by Sfera International in Milan
on Gardamatte paper.

1,000 soft cover copies for the
Herbert F. Johnson Museum of Art,
Cornell University

December 2002

*

After the first printing was sold out,
and after it was realized that Sfera International
had gone out of business and the original disks were lost,
1,000 soft cover copies
were printed and bound
by Archaeology & Art Publications
in Istanbul
(the project coordinated by Ahmet Başgelen)
for the Herbert F. Johnson Museum of Art,
and for Cornell University Press
September 2010

*

The publication costs of this volume
have been partially underwritten
by the Laistner Endowment of *Cornell
Studies in Classical Philology* and by
the Hull Memorial Publication Fund of
Cornell University.

Library of Congress Control Number: 2010938631
ISBN-13: 978-1-934260-08-1
ISBN-10: 1-934260-08-8

Published by:
Herbert F. Johnson Museum of Art
Cornell University
Ithaca, New York 14853
www.museum.cornell.edu

Printed in Turkey by:
Mega Print

Distributed by:
Cornell University Press
Ithaca, New York 14850
www.cornellpress.cornell.edu

Archaeology & Art Publications
Richmond, Indiana 47375
www.aapbl.com